BROKEN
But God

BROKEN
But God

A Powerful Message on Forgiving Your Abuser
While Restoring Your Life

Priscilla R. Haley

BROKEN BUT GOD
Published by Purposely Created Publishing Group™
Copyright © 2018 Priscilla R. Haley

All rights reserved.

No part of this book may be reproduced, distributed or transmitted in any form by any means, graphics, electronics, or mechanical, including photocopy, recording, taping, or by any information storage or retrieval system, without permission in writing from the publisher, except in the case of reprints in the context of reviews, quotes, or references.

Printed in the United States of America
ISBN: 978-1-947054-46-2

Special discounts are available on bulk quantity purchases by book clubs, associations and special interest groups. For details email: brokenbutgod2@gmail.com or call (817) 689-4071.

For information logon to:
www.brokenbutgod.com

DEDICATION

This book is dedicated to my beautiful daughter, Alexus Tamara, and my precious granddaughters, Nyla Jade, Kortne Janae, and Layiah Michelle. May each of you always walk in your queenship, know your worth, and never allow yourself to be mistreated or abused in any way. I was broken so that you will never have to be . . . but God.

For the millions of domestic violence victims in the world. I pray that this book will touch the life of at least one individual who reads it . . . be it the victim or the abuser . . . both need change in the right direction to move forward in the healing process. May God bless every reader of this book. For Psalm 126:5 encourages us, "those who sow with tears will reap with songs of joy!"

TABLE OF CONTENTS

Acknowledgments 1

Definition 4

Foreword 7

Introduction: Brokenness 11

CHAPTER 1:
Family Secrets 15

CHAPTER 2:
Stolen Innocence 27

CHAPTER 3:
Moving On 39

CHAPTER 4:
Didn't See It Coming 45

CHAPTER 5:
The Signs Were There 61

CHAPTER 6:
Traumas 71

CHAPTER 7:
Keep Your Friends Close and Your Enemies Closer 85

CHAPTER 8:
Anger 101

CHAPTER 9:
Love at First Sight 109

CHAPTER 10:
Clouds on the Horizon 121

CHAPTER 11:
That Christmas 131

CHAPTER 12:
The Breaking Point 137

CHAPTER 13:
Starting to Heal 147

CHAPTER 14:
After It's Over, It's Not Over 157

CHAPTER 15:
Freedom–The Power of Forgiveness 169

Resources 181

Prayers 185

Affirmations 191

Sources 193

ACKNOWLEDGMENTS

First and foremost, I would like to thank my amazing Heavenly Father God. I am amazed at the power of Your Name! I am amazed at the power of Your love for me! Thank you Father God that, in the process of putting this book together, I realized how true You are to Your word. Thank you for Your Amazing Grace! Thank you for the gift of writing. Thank you for giving me the power to believe in my passion and pursue my dreams, the calling You have on my life. I could never have done this without my unwavering faith, that fearless faith that I have in You, God Almighty.

To my beloved mother, although you're not here physically, your spiritual presence is what kept me going. For the first time in fifty-one years, I am speechless! I can barely find the words to express all the wisdom, love, and support you imparted in my life. You left your fingerprints of faith and love in my heart and for that I am eternally grateful. If I am blessed to live long enough, I hope I will be as good of a mother, grandmother, sister, and friend as you were to me. I love you, Mommy.

To my dad, the first man I ever loved. There will never be another dad quite like you. Your smile warms the hearts of all you come in contact with. I've watched in awe the example you set for your children. Your love and unwavering faith in God kept me afloat in some of my darkest moments. You didn't know all that I had gone through, and I intentionally withheld the dark secrets to protect you from protecting me. You never cease to amaze me! The life you've lived may not have produced millions of dollars, a fancy car, or beautiful homes, but what you've given to me is much more valuable than all of those material things: unconditional love and a heart for God. For that, I am thankful. My dad, my hero. I love you!

To my husband, Darin Haley, what can I say? Thank you for your amazing patience throughout my lengthy writing sessions over the last four years. You've been told "not right now, hold on babe, let me finish this last chapter," and more, but you hung in there and encouraged me to keep going. I am so thankful that I have you in my corner pushing me when I am ready to give up. All the good that comes from this book I look forward to sharing with you! Thanks for not just believing, but knowing that I could do this! I love you, always and forever!

A special thanks to Alexandria Barlowe. Thank you for helping me keep the creative juices flowing and bringing life to the essence of this project. I am forever grateful.

Last but not least, Emily Claudette Freeman. One of my favorite movies is *The Color Purple*. My favorite quote from that movie works here: "I want to thank you, Miss Celie, fo' everything you done for me. I 'members that day in the store with Miss Millie—I's feelin' real down. I's feelin' mighty bad. And when I see'd you—I know'd there is a God. I know'd there is a God." Thank you from the bottom of my heart. You took my thoughts and ran with them. You tugged at my heartstrings and pulled out memories that I wanted to forget. This book would not be so full of life and transparency without you pulling out the greatness you saw in me as a writer. I'm humbled and eternally grateful for you.

BRO-KEN
(Collins Dictionary)

Past participle of break

Subdued totally, humbled: a broken spirit

Crushed by grief: broken heart

Financially ruined: bankrupt

Sundered by separation or desertion: broken relationship

Not functioning, out of order: broken mentally

Having been violated: broken promises

BRO-KEN
(Priscilla's Dictionary)

It doesn't happen all at once.

You lose a piece here.

You lose a piece there.

You slip, you stumble, and you readjust your grip.

A few more pieces fall.

It happens so slowly.

You don't even realize you're broken . . .

until you already are.

FOREWORD

Merriam-Webster has a great deal to say about what it means to be broken. Specifically, it defines *broken* as "separated into parts or pieces by being hit or damaged, not working properly, and not kept or honored." Additionally, broken means "having undergone or been subjected to fracture; being irregular, interrupted, or full of obstacles; violated by transgression; made weak; subdued completely; reduced in rank; cut off;" and, lastly, "not complete or full."

If you are anything like me, you will have felt every part of that definition at some point or at many points in your life. Perhaps it was your childhood that left you feeling separated into parts or pieces. Maybe it was one of your parents; instead of loving you, caring for you, nurturing you, and protecting you, they damaged you with their words, actions, or inactions and left you "not working properly." Or maybe it was a sibling or older cousin. Did they say or do something to you that caused you to feel as if you had been subjected to a fracture and were therefore irregular? Maybe it was not your childhood. Maybe you had a wholesome home life as a child, and it was something or someone in your adulthood that has caused you to feel as if your happiness has been interrupted or filled with obstacles.

Psalm 34:18 (NKJV) tells us that "the Lord is near to those who have a broken heart, and saves such as have a contrite spirit." Aren't we so blessed to have God near to us when we feel as if we are the very definition of broken? If, as you read these words, you feel like your picture should be next to *broken* in the dictionary, this book is just for you! I am so glad that God directed you to it.

Priscilla is a dear friend of mine and I am truly proud of the way she has allowed God to work in her and heal her brokenness. As you read her story and testimony, rest assured that you are not alone. There are countless broken people walking about this Earth. Thankfully, Priscilla is someone who did not want to stay broken! She prayed, cried, and stayed steadfast before God's face until her pieces were mended. She has now made it her mission to help other women who are in broken places. In her story, you will find that Priscilla is transparent about the ups and downs and the many levels of brokenness that she has faced. It is my prayer that you will use her testimony as a cloud of witness against all negativity. It is my prayer that you, too, decide to begin the process of mending your brokenness.

In my darkest hour, there were times when I was so hurt, devastated, and broken that I felt as if I could not breathe. Life can take us there sometimes! Can you relate? If so, please be encouraged. Please lift your head and keep it held high. Even if there are tears streaming down your face, hold your head high! You are the righteousness of God. He called you, predestined you, and graced you for a time such as this. His word tells us in Psalm 147:3 (NKJV), "He heals the brokenhearted and binds up their wounds." I encourage you to allow God's word to be a healing balm and soothing elixir for your deepest and darkest hurts. God loves you and He wants nothing more than for you to be healed. He wants to restore every broken area in your life so that you can fully walk in His purpose and on His path for your life. Trust me—that purpose is not for you to remain broken, for He gets no glory in that. His glory comes when you are healed and help others to do the same!

I am so excited for the awesome and miraculous things that are in store for your life! We know that Romans 8:28 tells us that *all* things work together for the good of those that love Him. Of course, it is much easier said than done, but please understand that even your most painful experiences are working for your own good! I pray that you feel the warmth and love of God's embrace as you read each page of this book. I pray that you allow Priscilla's testimony to resonate with your spirit. I pray that you have the courage to recognize the things in your life that cause you to feel broken. I pray that God removes any person or thing that is unlike Him so that you can truly flourish. Most importantly, I pray that you realize that, regardless of what caused you to be broken, there is a *But God* moment that awaits you! I love you and I am praying for and with you always!

God Bless,

Cheryl Polote-Williamson,
Author, Speaker, and Entrepreneur

BROKENNESS

Brokenness is God's way of breaking us away from self-reliance and the desire to act independently of Him. There is a holy purpose in being broken. God uses His breaking process to transform, strengthen, and bless us. He wants to bring every broken area in our lives under submission for His will to be done, and He uses our trials to lead us to a place of total surrender.

Our Father will often use adversity to break our self-will and transform us into useful vessels for His kingdom. While going through the trials in my life, all I could focus on was the pain and the hardships. What I failed to realize then was that there was purpose in that pain. God was speaking and trying to break through my self-will so that I would turn my focus to Him and be completely devoted to allowing His will, not mine, to be done.

Being broken was not my punishment. It was God showing me His mercy with the intent that I repent and turn from my wicked ways. There was physical, emotional, verbal, sexual, and relational pain and suffering in my surrender to God. But the blessings that have come on the other side of my brokenness are worth it, and I would not trade my journey for anything.

I write this book for every empty-eyed girl with tears and trembling lips, struggling to mention the unmentionable. I write to the quivering voices of broken women who have finally spoken the secret they could not keep and would not tell. I write to every husband who holds his wife tightly at night . . . a little girl lost in space, a rosebud crushed before he ever met her, a broken soul shaking in his arms. I write to my sisters who hide behind silk dresses and designer handbags, bearing a terrible shame that their Mac makeup cannot cover and cold showers cannot wash away.

Some call them abused women. Some called them victims. Some even call them statistics. But I call them *broken*. These broken women come in all colors and forms. Black and white, rich and poor. Often camouflaged behind the walls of otherwise-successful lives, people who wrestle with secret pain.

You, my sister, may be one of them. You may not show any outward signs of trauma, but your tragedy might have destroyed your life had God not held you together. God can greatly use you to restore wholeness to others who walk in varying degrees of brokenness.

Every time you see an insecure, vulnerable, intimidated adult woman with unnatural fear in her eyes, low self-esteem, or an apologetic posture, you may be staring at a woman who has been broken. When you look closely into her eyes, you may see a woman who has been bruised, weakened, hurt, maimed, or disturbed . . . but God. To them and to you, I say: The power to heal is in the power to care. Compassion is the mother of all miracles.

If you yourself are broken, I say: Allow someone into your life who can fix what's wrong. The walls you have built to protect yourself have also imprisoned you, but God wants to release you from the dungeon of fear. He wants you to rise and be healed in the name of Jesus—and so do I.

Priscilla R. Haley,

Broken—but God!

Chapter 1
FAMILY SECRETS

"Robert, STOP!" my aunt Agnes yelled, lifting both arms to shield her face from yet another violent swing of his steel-toed work boot.

"I'll stop when you've learned your lesson!" he shouted angrily.

He looked like a rabid dog on the loose. I stood conflicted, stuck between being frozen in fear and desperately wanting to pull him off my aunt Agnes. He was much too strong and my ten-year-old muscles were no worthy opponent for his drunken rage. I kept trying to figure out what she could have done to make him so angry. What could she possibly have said to make him feel that the only solution was to repeatedly bash her over the head with his five-pound boot?

When he finally grew weary of beating my dearest aunt, he stormed out, slamming the door as he left. As if nearly beating her to death wasn't enough, he had to leave with a bang as well (pun intended). We wept as I helped Aunt Agnes wipe the blood from her face and bandage her wounds. I tried to hug her as tight as I could. She squeezed back, sobbing so hard that I could feel her ribs shifting with every whimper. In that moment, I promised myself that I would never allow a man to hurt me that way.

That would be a promise I wouldn't keep . . .

I grew up in a family that revered God in every way. We attended Sunday school and church every week at St. Peter Baptist Church, a little old red brick church that sat off E. Dalzell Street and Youree Drive in Shreveport, the third largest city in Louisiana, sitting alongside the Red River. Growing up in Shreveport also meant growing up in God for my family, so I went through my younger years practicing with the youth choir and participating in every program and play that was produced for the congregation.

I recall happily welcoming the month of May each year because it meant Jolly Bible Time was coming. Jolly Bible Time was a Joy Bus ministry at Creswell Church of Christ, on the corner of Creswell and Kirby Street. I can remember the big white bus slowly driving down our street, stopping at every other home. As the kids approached the bus—with big bold letters that read "Jolly Bible Time"—my eyes would light up. This was an exciting time for me because it showed me that no matter the color of your skin, we all served the same God. This lesson was especially emphasized for me because

Jolly Bible Time was started by white folks who took it upon themselves to come into many black communities throughout Shreveport and shuttle us to church. There was a song that is still dear to me that we always sang on the bus: "I am happy today, oh yes, I'm happy today. In Jesus Christ, I'm happy today. Because He's taken all of my sins away and that's why I'm happy today." We would sing that song until our hearts were truly full of joy!

My life was good. Not many kids in our neighborhood were afforded birthday parties and summer vacations like we were. My mother would typically buy matching outfits for the girls and find a coordinating-color outfit for my brother. She almost always made sure she had film in her Polaroid to capture any and every defining and memorable moment. When picture day at school would roll around, Mom would make sure that we were the best dressed in our class. We would have new outfits and perfectly combed hair, with fancy bows that her friend Rosie made for us. She would then grab her camera and snap away. She had to have the first picture for every occasion. Christmas, Easter, Mother's Day, Father's Day, family vacations—it didn't matter; Mom and her Polaroid were going to capture it.

We lived in a three-bedroom, modest home at 536 Lomax Street. My mother single-handedly served as the interior decorator, showcasing her great taste in décor and design and creating a home her family could be comfortable in. The living room was finished with an English-style brown, gold, and light blue paisley sofa with a matching love seat, accompanied by light brown chaise chairs. The coffee table and end tables were adorned with tall lamps that had oversized beige shades. The living room was off-limits to the children and used only when Mom was entertaining her friends. The walls were nicely decorated with pictures and shiny brass sconces. Our life growing up was good—on the surface.

Mom was devoted to our family. She was the CEO and the disciplinarian in our home. My siblings and I knew when she meant business. She had the ability to straighten us up with one stern look. She taught us the importance of family and sticking together very early on in our lives. She would always tell us that she wanted us to be so close that one couldn't fall without the others falling as well. I literally took that to heart.

"Your family is all you've got. Don't ever forget that," she would always say. My grandmother would say the same thing at family gatherings. They put so much emphasis on family that one would be remiss to think any other way.

My dad was the leader and provider of our family. He always treated our mom with respect and love. I knew that he and Mom argued from time to time, but I never saw my dad hit my mom or speak to her in a disrespectful manner. Dad worked and brought his paycheck home. Mom took care of the household. Seemed simple.

We discovered, however, that things weren't as they seemed. Dad started drinking a lot. Then he started staying out later than usual. Mom's demeanor changed. She was angry with Dad all the time, and it seemed as if she were angry at the world. Then the arguments started. I could sense our life as we knew it was about to change.

One afternoon I came home from school and Mom was sitting at the kitchen table smoking her Salem Lights. She seemed calm, but I knew something was brewing. That night, when Dad came in from work, all hell broke loose. Mom accused him of having an affair with the aunt of my brother's best friend. He didn't deny it. I was devastated. How could he do this to our family?

I struggled to understand why my father would do this to my mom. Why had he been drinking so much? What had Mom done to make him want to seek comfort in another woman? Was it us or was it just life? My dad never knew his father, and when I would ask him how he felt about it, he would calmly say, "I made it this far without him, I don't need him now." I often wonder if that had something to do with him self-medicating all those years with alcohol and looking elsewhere for love. Even now, those questions remain, and I am rarely comfortable when searching within myself to understand. My mom tried to tough it out for years, but in 1983 she had had enough. She packed up her things and ours and we left. My life changed forever. I was angry; angry with my dad for forcing my mother to leave because of his womanizing ways and angry with my mother for not trying to make it work. We moved in with my grandmother, though I didn't want to leave the only place I knew as home. Dad continued to live in the house, but his wandering ways soon caught up with him.

Bam! Bam! Bam! It sounded as if the police were ramming my grandmother's door with something. I jumped off the sofa where I had been peacefully sleeping. My sister Audrey ran in from the back room. When she swung the door open, there stood Cynthia, the daughter of Dad's friend Louis. She looked uncertain as she nervously placed all her weight on one leg.

"Priscilla," she stammered. "Um . . . y'all's daddy is hurt. Um . . . Ms. Betty's brothers jumped him bad and I think y'all need to go check on him."

My eyes bulged and tears started forming as Audrey demanded answers. "How do you know all this?"

Cynthia responded, "Victor told me." Victor was the son of another woman that my dad had been seeing while he was cheating on my mother with Betty. Dad was cheating on all of them.

My little brother staggered to the door and behind him stood my mom. "What's going on?" she asked. I couldn't speak. The task of repeating the story became Cynthia's.

My mother showed no emotion. She looked at us and said, "Y'all go see about your dad." We got dressed and headed out the door for the five-minute walk to our old home. As we approached the back door, there was no sign of anyone. When we got closer, though, it was clear something was wrong because the door was slightly ajar. It was pitch dark, so I slowly pushed the door open and hit the light switch on the wall. Nothing happened. I flicked the switch several times--nothing. I looked back at my sister and, just as we were about to back out of the house, we heard a loud moan coming from the living room.

I rushed through the dark to the living room, where the moaning was coming from, while Audrey, who had gone out the back door, came running in through the front.

"Oh, Lord!" my dad was screaming.

Audrey tried to turn the light switch on in the living room, hoping it would work where the first switch had not. We went from one end of the living room to the other, trying to turn the lamps on—nothing.

"Dad, what happened to you?" I asked. He was moaning and groaning loudly. Audrey found a cigarette lighter on the table near Dad and flicked it on. We both started screaming.

"Call the police!" Audrey yelled.

I fumbled my way back to the kitchen and grabbed the receiver of the phone mounted on the wall, dialing 911. It seemed like it took forever for the ambulance to arrive. We found towels and placed them on Dad's head to stop the bleeding. He was a bloody mess. By the time the ambulance arrived, it seemed as if the entire neighborhood were standing around trying to see what was going on. The people from the ambulance rushed us out of the house and set up flashlights so they could tend to my dad. I was a nervous wreck. My sister and I sat on the front steps, sobbing, our clothes covered in our dad's blood. My mom and grandmother made their way to the house just as the paramedics were closing the door to the ambulance.

Again, my mom showed no emotion. She told us to go inside and we obeyed. I reached for the light switch again, but still nothing. It had become obvious by that point that the electricity had been turned off. My mom had her cigarette lighter, so she made her way to the kitchen and pulled out a box of candles. Carefully lighting them one by one, she passed them to me and my sister. As we strategically placed the candles in the holders throughout the living room and the kitchen, our eyes grew wider than dessert plates at the amount of blood on the floor. Mom's couch was drenched. She stared, motionless. Her lips quivered and tears rolled down her face. I couldn't tell if she was crying for Dad or at the fact that her beautiful sofa was ruined.

She took a couple of candles and walked to the back of the house, with us silently following her. There were no signs that Dad had even been sleeping in the bed. Everything seemed to be in place, just as she had left it months ago. The entire incident had a profound effect on my understanding of life.

At the age of twelve, years before this, my innocence was snatched away from me; finding my father in such a way further traumatized my life through the end of high school. My mother filed for divorce, which killed all hope of my parents ever reconciling. Mom did her best to keep us unaware of the details regarding our father, but facts kept coming through to us all the same. One of my clearest memories is hiding in my grandmother's closet after I had stolen a dollar to go to Ms. Pearl to buy peanut patties. While I was waiting for the coast to be clear, I overheard Mom talking with Grandma, telling her that Dad had fathered another child while they were married. Another bombshell dropped!

I couldn't move. I had lost my appetite for the old-fashioned, homemade peanut patties. I felt remorse for even stealing the dollar to buy them. I sat in the closet, waiting for the opportune time to carefully stuff the dollar back in Grandma's coin purse. When the coast was finally clear, I slowly slid from behind the curtain that covered the closet door. There was no sign of my mom or my grandma, which made it easy for me to put the dollar back.

I often wonder if my anger at my mom for not trying to stick it out with my dad after his infidelity is what led me to accept such egregious behaviors in my own relationships. Did I consciously choose to stay in relationships out of fear of the outcome? How was it that I couldn't walk away like my mom did, but instead set an incredibly low standard for what was acceptable in my relationships?

My reality of what it meant to trust and be loyal to the end would prove to be a series of life-shattering and life-changing experiences.

Seeing Aunt Agnes's boyfriend beat her that night was the first time I ever witnessed a man hit a woman. She and I shared a special bond, so it was difficult to see her treated that way. Like Mom, my aunt was very family-oriented. My grandmother had set the tone for that mindset.

As I got older, I realized that the women in my family, especially my grandmother, never wanted to address certain situations that happened in the family. Grandmother was very secretive when it came to alcohol and drug addictions, while affairs, mistakes, abusive behavior, and other problems were always dismissed and excused away. The women in my life seemed to believe that keeping the secrets would save them from experiencing the pain of knowing. Many families still feel the same as my grandmother about airing the family's dirty laundry. I understand that these secret matters have shame attached to them, but not knowing kept me out of the loop and had a devastating effect on my life as a young girl. The thing about secrets is that, sooner or later, they will be revealed.

"What happens in this house stays in this house." My grandma repeated this mantra often. I wondered why she always expressed that so sternly to me. Did she know something I didn't? Or perhaps it was because I had been labeled a "motor mouth" for being so talkative. I would ask for an explanation of an explanation, and then more explanations after that. I was the inquisitive one. Always wanting to know more than anyone was willing to share.

I remember my uncle Ernest once jumped on my aunt Reese at my grandmother's house. Aunt Reese had run to the phone and was trying to call the police when my grandmother snatched the phone out of her hands and sternly told her, "We don't bother other people with our problems. In a marriage, you go through things, you work it out, you live to see another day."

My aunt stopped dead in her tracks. The next day, it was as if nothing had ever happened. I was stunned at my grandmother's reaction. Your daughter gets pounced on by her husband and you choose to protect him—not her. This would go on for years. I would see one aunt after another enduring some form of abuse—emotional, mental, physical, or verbal. It happened, and it happened more than I care to voice.

I once asked my mom why. Why did Grandma protect the men in the family? Why did she uphold them in their wrongdoing? But I never got a reply.

I was the one who questioned everything, including why we had to keep secrets. This trait of secrecy seemed to have been passed down to my mother, and I figured it would eventually take its rightful place in my life as well, that I would eventually understand. Now, I often wish that the women in my life had been strong enough to tackle our family issues head-on. I wish they would have recognized the dangers of covering up our bone-chilling family secrets. If only they would have talked to us openly about the abuse, if only we had been educated about certain behaviors instead of cautiously sweeping them under the rug, we could have possibly avoided a lot of unnecessary pain. This cloak of family secrecy has proven to be a toxic force in my life. It prevented me from being able to trust and openly communicate with others. As an adult, I resolved to snatch up that rug, throw it out, and carefully clean up each painful piece of dirt left behind by generational curses and family secrets that have haunted the very essence of my soul.

Chapter 2
STOLEN INNOCENCE

It was the summer of 1978. The weather was nice and the sun was shining brightly in Seattle. My mom had resolved to make this our vacation destination that year. This would be the summer that would drastically change my life. I was an inquisitive twelve-year-old girl who was overly excited about the three-day bus trip with my siblings, eager to see other parts of the country. I remember fighting with my little brother for the window seat. "Move," my little brother Frank insisted, as his little hands tried to pull me out of the seat.

Mom gave me *that* look and I knew I had to succumb and let him have the window seat. It did make him quite happy—the toothless grin on his face said it all. I really wanted to sit by the window, but I also knew that, because I was taller than he was, I would still be able to see out the window just as well, so it was okay.

The driver made one last announcement that the bus was preparing to depart to Seattle, Washington. Mom had packed coloring books, crayons, reading books, and puzzle-activity books for us. We had what looked like a mini grocery store stored in the overhead bins and a little white Styrofoam cooler filled with juice, soda, water, ham, cheese, and fried chicken. Mom was prepared. We would go from Shreveport to Longview, Texas, and then on to Dallas. From Dallas, we would make the rest of the long journey to Seattle.

I stared out of the window the entire trip. I enjoyed seeing the beauty of God's creation as we journeyed from one state to another, dropping off and picking up passengers frequently. When the driver spoke into the loudspeaker on the third day, I had a smile as wide as the sea.

"Welcome to Seattle, Washington," he said in a deep, Barry White tone. You could hear the passengers rumbling about, trying to gather their belongings. It had been a long three-day trip for many of us. My mom had us sit quietly while she checked our surroundings to make sure no trash or personal belongings lingered anywhere. Mom had a thing for cleanliness; it didn't matter if it was a bus ride or a bathroom, she made sure everything was always clean and in order.

One by one the passengers exited the bus with excitement, searching through the crowd for their loved ones. We were almost the last ones to get off. My mom led the way, like a mother duck leading her ducklings. Once we were all accounted for, Mom led us through the crowd to this big, long, shiny green station wagon trimmed in brown and beige. It reminded me of ours back in Shreveport. I smiled as we got near.

My sisters and I were making jokes and goofy eyes at each other. My uncle Clarence was sitting on the front hood of the car, smoking a cigarette. As we got closer to the car, I could see a couple of young guys sitting in the back. It was my cousin Marcus and his friend Larry. They looked weird and too old. It was four of us plus them designated to sit in the back of the station wagon. How were we all going to fit? After Uncle Clarence stuffed our luggage and blankets in the back, my little brother was put in the front seat with my mom. My sisters and I were stuffed in the back with the two musty boys. The stench left an unforgettable impression, a combination of smoke and musk . . . ugh. Marcus was staring at me like he had seen a ghost or something. "Lord, how long is this ride going to take?" I mumbled as I tried to inhale through the stench between us.

The drive would only took about twenty-five minutes or so, and before we knew it, we were pulling up in front of the big-framed house. The yard was huge and there were at least ten concrete steps to climb. My aunt Clara stood in the doorway with her flowered duster on, smiling from ear to ear. She swung the door open as my mom approached and embraced her for what seemed like forever. And then, one by one, we entered the house as Aunt Clara hugged and kissed us. The aroma coming from the kitchen filled the house. My aunt Clara loved to entertain and she really loved to cook and feed the hungry, which is exactly what we were—hungry. We would have to wait just a few more hours to dive into those pots.

The adults settled in the dining room and my mom instructed us to go outside and play. Once outside, my sister and I looked at each other, as if to say, "Now what?" The weather was fair. On the neighbor's side of the street, there were blocks that had been lightly chalked for hopscotch—one of our favorite pastimes at home, along with a good game of jacks. My little sister shouted, "Hopscotch," and so it was.

We must have jumped for hours. The weather was just right. Not too hot and not too cool. Although Seattle is notorious for its gloomy and rainy weather, that day was anything but. As the day came to an end and we gathered in the house for dinner, I felt a sense of uneasiness come over me as Marcus peered at me with bloodshot eyes. It was the same look he had given me on the way home from the bus station. What's wrong with him? I asked myself. I quickly turned my attention to all the chatter going on at the other end of the table.

My aunt Clara and my mom were still trading stories of their lucky finds at garage sales and local Goodwill stores. Aunt Clara and Mom seemed to be so engrossed with the bag of goodies that they had purchased earlier that day from their favorite Goodwill store that they hardly noticed what was going on at the other end of the table.

I tried to look engaged, but it was difficult because Marcus was sitting directly across from me. You know that feeling you get when you're being stared at? Out of the corner of my eye, just outside my field of vision, I could feel him peering at me.

Something wasn't right. I felt sick to my stomach. My deep feeling of relief when he excused himself from the table was indescribable.

Later that evening, we had all settled in and found our pallets—blankets and quilts folded to resemble sleeping bag-like little mattresses—on the living room floor. I was excited because it looked like a big campground right there inside Aunt Clara's living room. We all laid on the floor watching television, as children like to do, with the warmth from the soft carpet beneath me making me feel cozy and safe. We all snickered and giggled at the character Arnold from the TV sitcom *Diff'rent Strokes*. The tagline "What you talkin' 'bout, Willis?" had us rolling on the floor. After a few hours of *Diff'rent Strokes* and *Mork and Mindy*, it was lights out.

The television that had roared so loudly was silenced. I awoke to my cousin Marcus holding one hand over my mouth while pinning me down with the other. He wasn't a big guy, but he was big and forceful enough to hold my boney little frame down. I was frozen with fear, intimidated. I absolutely could not move a muscle. He was tugging at my underwear. It was the middle of the night; I was half asleep and thought I must be dreaming. It didn't feel real, it didn't make any sense. Where was everyone? Where were my sisters? Why was he doing this to me?

It was all over quickly, and as fast as he appeared, he disappeared. He had used his finger to forcefully assault me. I laid there and clung to every thread in the carpet I could find for comfort. I slowly lifted my head to see where everyone had gone, only to find they were there, sound asleep. What just happened? I kept asking myself, too afraid to move. A burning sensation had crept in and I was scared. What if he came back? Unable to go to sleep, I laid there in silence until I could see a glimpse of the morning sun.

I was slow to get up that morning. Everyone had gotten up except me, until finally my mom came in to roust me out of bed. I knew I had no choice but to get up. I dragged myself up with the cover around my waist to hide my soiled nightgown. I had peed on myself during the night. It would be a recurring problem for the next few years. I started asking myself, what had I done or said to make him do this? Had I done something to encourage this? And then I thought, was this rape, even though he had used his finger only? This was my cousin. This was family. My head was spinning and I felt physically sick to my stomach again.

I did nothing that day. I tried to stay as close to my mom as possible. That wouldn't last long, because we were not allowed to be in the company of adults when they were talking. On this day, though, I took a chance and sat on the other side of the dining room, out of view. I listened to my mom and Aunt Clara as they talked about family issues, things my twelve-year-old ears had no business hearing. But my hiding spot was suddenly revealed.

"What are you doing back here?" my cousin Shelia asked.

"Who is back there?" yelled Aunt Clara.

Shelia replied, "Priscilla is sitting in here on the floor."

My eyes got as big as silver dollars. I had been instructed to go outside with the others and I had failed to obey. My mom called me to the room and asked why I was in the house. I couldn't speak. She asked me again, but still I couldn't speak. I don't know where she found the ruler, but she took to my lips with it.

"So, you can't answer when I'm talking to you?" She slapped my lips with the ruler repeatedly.

I refused to cry in front of the adults. I guess Mom finally realized she was literally beating a dead horse and stopped. She instructed me again to go outside, and this time, I obeyed. I sat on the front porch and watched my siblings playing hide-and-go-seek with the neighbors' kids. I was too sore to run and play. I was consumed with the thoughts of what had happened the night before. I didn't know what to think or say. Everybody seemed to be normal except me. What if I told them? They will never believe me, I kept telling myself. This was my aunt Clara's son, my first cousin. This was their home. I immediately began to blame myself. Maybe I should have slept in the middle instead of wanting to sleep near the bathroom. What if, what if, what if, I kept asking myself. I began to blame myself again. My mind could not comprehend this whole scenario, so to cope with it, I blocked it out as if it had never happened. I shut down completely and made the decision to never tell a soul.

The next night we all found our spots on the living room floor again. But after everyone else was asleep, the horror show from the night before started playing again.

"Marcus," I gasped, "What are you doing in here?" He looked at me again with those same bloodshot eyes.

"Be quiet," he grunted.

I closed my eyes and pleaded within—Lord, not again. I felt violated all over again. I was petrified. This time was even more terrifying, because now, he was face-to-face with me.

"Be quiet," Marcus said again, harshly, as he began to stroke my thigh. I tried to inch away, but he pulled me closer to him.

"Stop touching me," I mumbled. He yanked my hair, causing my neck to pop. I whimpered and complied with his commands to be quiet. Fearing what he would do next, I tried to cross my legs, but he quickly placed his leg in between mine. I froze. "Stop," I whimpered again.

I had no idea what he was doing as he began to pull at my nightgown, but this time, unlike the night before, I knew that things would quickly become worse. I squirmed and tried to move away to keep him from touching me. He was persistent, and the more I moved, the more aggressive he became. I groaned loudly, thinking he would leave if the others might wake, but he didn't. I tried to stick my leg out and kick my sister who was lying near to me. I knew that if I could get her attention she would help get him off me. Unfortunately, I could not reach her. I felt like a ghost, kicking and mumbling while everyone around me slept. Before I could do anything to stop him, he violated me.

He hurt me so deeply that all I could do was cry. I prayed that it would be over soon as I lay there crying and in shock. Why was he doing this to me? I had so many questions and I was in so much pain. When he finally got off me, I picked myself up and ran to the bathroom, crying quietly. I felt so dirty, violated, betrayed, and embarrassed. As I sat on the toilet, crying, I saw blood and decided to shower. I tried to scrub the dirty feeling away, but all the scrubbing in the world could not undo that awful feeling. I finished cleaning myself and tried my best to stop crying. I dried myself off and walked, shaking, back to my pallet. I prayed that no one would hear me. I was so ashamed.

I began to wonder what I had done to deserve something so hurtful. Did I say something or do something to make him think I wanted this? With all six of us sprawled out across the living room floor that night, why me? Why didn't anyone hear or see what was going on? Or did they? Was this what Grandma was talking about when she said, "What goes on in this house, stays in this house"? I was emotionally and physically exhausted. I wanted nothing more than to silence the millions of thoughts swimming around in my head. Unfortunately, I was powerless to stop them. I cried myself to sleep that night.

The next morning, we all gathered for breakfast in the family dining room. I avoided making eye contact with everyone, especially him. He sneered at me as if I had done something wrong. When no one was looking, he got up and walked over to me. As he moved in my direction, every muscle in my body froze.

"You better keep your mouth shut. No one is going to believe you if you tell. They will think you wanted it. Don't say a word," he whispered cruelly. "You are a big girl now so it's time you start acting like it."

Tears began to form but I quickly wiped them away. I believed him. Everyone would think something was wrong with me if I told them. So, I followed his instructions and kept my mouth shut. I also kept thinking about what Grandma had said. I knew that I could not tell a soul, so I didn't. I walked around with so much hurt and shame after that evening. It's almost as if that horrible night marked the end of my childhood. I couldn't help but ask myself, Why did that have to happen to me? What kind of monster would do that to their own flesh and blood? Had he done this to any of my other cousins or my sisters? These questions swirled around in my head for decades. My heartbreak reached new levels when I learned that he had, in fact, done the same to my sister. I wept for her and for me. I wished so desperately that I could have told someone. I felt like keeping this dark secret was doing more harm than good. After all, if my family knew that this had happened, they could have perhaps stopped him from doing it again. But year after year, when I thought about it, Grandmother's voice would ring loudly in my ears: "Whatever happens in this house, stays in this house. Family is all you've got." My heart ached and I hated him for placing me in this prison of secrecy and for stealing my innocence.

After everyone cleared their plates, I sat quietly at the table, alone. It was as if I were invisible. No one seemed to notice I was sitting there. The tears began to well up in my eyes and I began to question God: Why did You let this happen? Why didn't You stop him? I was angry and had a bone to pick with God. I would spend the remaining days of our vacation feeling helpless and carrying a burden that wasn't mine to carry. It became another family secret. For years I blamed myself. No matter what I did or how many friends I surrounded myself with, I always felt alone. I thought I was the only one with a dark family secret. The rape and then the trauma haunted me for years. While my body had healed, my thought process and inner core had been deeply damaged. Because I blamed myself, I hated myself. I was terrified to sleep alone at night. I had bouts of bed-wetting. The events of that summer vacation continued to torture me every minute of every day.

Chapter 3
MOVING ON

In Shreveport, where I grew up, many of the parents in our neighborhood were good friends. Everyone looked out for one another and our elders were highly respected. As children, we knew we had to walk a fine line, because my parents had given all the neighborhood permission to tear into us if they saw us out of order. And once they told my mom, we got disciplined again. So, we got double for our trouble, as the old saying goes. A lot of my friends smoked pot and cigarettes, and alcohol was pervasive amongst teens in the latter part of the 1970s (at least in Louisiana.) I didn't partake and I was treated like an outcast for being such a square.

We were the generation that watched *The Dating Game* and *The Brady Bunch*, Saturday morning cartoons and "Afternoon Specials"—after-school TV movies made for kids and teens. There weren't a lot of great shows on TV so we all watched the best ones on the same night and talked about them the next day.

We were given a lot of opportunities to explore the world on our own. We walked to our friends' houses or to the store, alone, and no one thought much about it. We weren't told to always walk with a friend, although my trips were usually with my sisters or a cousin. AIDS wasn't known yet and we ran free. The biggest thing we were warned about was herpes. This sexually transmitted disease was considered the worst thing that could happen to you for having sex, and my sisters and I learned about it from our aunt Connie. Mom didn't talk to us about sex. Her only conversation about the topic was one line: "If you get pregnant, you're going to have it."

That was a scary thought. I stayed as far away from boys and sex as I possibly could, especially after being assaulted by my cousin. I was this tall, lanky girl with full lips who could run a mile a minute and talk even faster. I loved football and track and field. I didn't find TV stars very impressive. A lot of girls looked to Farrah Fawcett for tips on how to do our hair, but while I had a good deal of lengthy hair and tried "feathering" it a couple of times, that was not the right style for me. I was taller than my sisters so I couldn't wear their clothes, but that didn't stop my mom from dressing us alike for family pictures.

Life growing up was adventurous at times. My mom made sure we celebrated birthdays and all holidays. Sometimes we celebrated simply to celebrate. Mom would fire up the grill, and the next thing you knew, the backyard was full of family and friends. My sisters and I were like three peas in a pod. We stuck together like glue. There was no internet at the time, but we sure had our share of phone conversations. I remember our hefty black phone with the silver circles that took two seconds to connect for each dial tone. Oh, how I laugh at those days sometimes. I grew up in Shreveport—but then I grew tired of it.

I developed an overwhelming desire to leave my hometown. I wanted to live a good life and have access to bigger and better opportunities. I felt that I could not do that in little old Shreveport, so I devised a plan to leave and venture out to a big city. Previously I had enrolled in the Southern University, with an emphasis in Business. After a few months of struggling with all my classes, though, I knew I needed to make a change. By the time I was nineteen, I was finally able to put my plan to attend a different school into action. I packed up what few belongings I had and left. I planned to stay with Aunt Clara in Seattle. In the weeks before I left, I was worried that I would be emotional and afraid to leave my family behind. Mama had her reservations and initially did not want me to leave, but she eventually came around and supported my decision to relocate. She promised that she would visit as much as she could. When the big day arrived, I was surprisingly not emotional at all. I was very excited to be able to leave and looked forward to all that Washington had to offer me now that I was older.

When I arrived in Washington, the first thing I noticed was the mountains. There were so many breathtakingly beautiful mountains. I had never lived in such a beautiful place.

I could get used to this, I thought. I was so excited to be in a new city. I was like a little sponge soaking in all the new scenery and the fresh air that marked a new beginning for me. I did have to adjust to the amount of rain there. At times, all the rain tended to be a bit depressing. Other than that, I was over the moon!

It wasn't until I moved to Seattle that I found out my cousin Lynn had been molested at the hands of my uncle—her father. The father of the cousin who had stolen my innocence at the age of twelve. They do say the apple doesn't fall too far from the tree. The monster I had portrayed him to be all those years was in fact a product of his father. I wondered, was sexual assault a part of his DNA? I tried to figure out how and why a father would commit the reprehensible act of taking advantage of his own daughter. Lynn said it started as early as the age of eight. It would go on for years until she ran away at fifteen and got married. My heart ached as my mind drifted back to those nights Marcus had violated me. Was he a victim of his own circumstances?

Trust was very difficult for me after being sexually assaulted by my cousin. After having fallen victim to such a horrendous act, I couldn't trust anyone, not even myself. Can you imagine the feeling of not being able to trust yourself? In order to understand why, you need to consider the misconceptions that I had. When it happened to me, I was young and cute, so I thought it was a sexually motivated act. I thought that, even though I was totally disinterested in boys, I must have done something to prompt it, that it must have somehow been my fault. I began to try and separate what Marcus had done from who he was. Marcus had gotten married and had three children by the time I moved to Seattle. Because my fresh start was so important to me, I tried to bury the thought that Marcus would hurt me again. Every Sunday, my aunt Clara had dinner after church at her home. I would get chills when he arrived with his family. Initially, every time I saw him, I felt like I had been hit by a Mack truck. I kept my distance, yet his presence would bring back memories and I would feel guilty all over again.

A few weeks after my relocation, I was somewhat settled in and ready to find a job. This was a bit challenging since I did not have a college degree, but I was determined to find whatever I could and make the best of it. My cousin Linda helped me get a position at her job, working as a housekeeper in a fancy hotel in downtown Seattle. It wasn't what I wanted, but it was a start. Certainly not what I envisioned my new life in the big city would be. Yet, I was going to start somewhere and make it work. Before long, I landed a better job as a bank teller at Washington Mutual Bank.

I enjoyed working at the bank and meeting new people. There were opportunities for advancement and they offered decent benefits. Things were starting to look up and my move to Seattle seemed to be the best move ever. My relationship with my aunt had blossomed, and it was as if my mom was in the background, whispering the things she would tell me. It was eerie at times. My aunt and my mom shared a lot of the same views when it came to life experiences. Aunt Clara would have a profound impact on my entire life. Living with her and watching how she chased after God would bind us together for eternity. She had a heart for God and was truly a giver to everyone she encountered. She would give the shirt off her back to anyone in need. Her kindness and generosity would soon rub off on me. I think she used Luke 6:38 (NIV) as a model for her life: "Give, and it will be given to you. A good measure, pressed down, shaken together and running over, will be poured into your lap. For with the measure you use, it will be measured to you."

My aunt Clara would always use scripture to drive a point home. It intrigued me at times, because I would often wonder if the scripture reference was being applied to something going on in her life or if she just needed to reinforce the word of God in mine. Nevertheless, my life was centered on God, and would remain so as long as I lived under Aunt Clara's roof.

Chapter 4
DIDN'T SEE IT COMING

He was the nice guy who lived across the street. I wasn't attracted to him at all, but his persistence was appealing to me for some reason. We started quickly. I met David when I was nineteen years old. He was nine years my senior. I was used to dating muscular guys who were much taller than me and close to my age. David was almost eye to eye with me and not physically fit at all. He was sporting a curly perm. I preferred bald men with full beards. I hadn't really gone out on the dating scene since arriving in Seattle, so I guess you can say I settled. I was young and dumb and he was the first guy to show interest in me after I left home. I was trying to be grown, as the old folks would say. My mom would say I was being fast.

After a few weeks, David had won me over. I succumbed to the slick-talking older man. He would wine and dine me, something I wasn't accustomed to, which made me feel special. Being so far away from home and feeling like no one was watching over me gave me a sense of independence. Hanging out, going to concerts, dancing, and drinking were routine date nights for us. I remember the first concert he took me to was the R&B group the Whispers. We moved and grooved to the loud sounds of "Rock Steady." We ended the night grabbing a late-night, two-piece dinner from the famous Ezell's Chicken. Ezell's, in the Central District off Twenty-Third Avenue, hit the map in later years after the entertainment mogul Oprah Winfrey requested they cater for her birthday, back in the early nineties.

Times were good in the beginning. Hanging out with David and his friends, who were all older than me, made me feel mature, engaging in grown-folk conversations and sipping on glasses of wine. Yes, I was drinking at the age of nineteen. I wasn't drinking heavy liquor; wine and wine coolers were my drinks of choice. They were sweet and didn't really have a lasting effect. David had a friend who played in the NFL whose wife I would eventually befriend. Janice was very pretty. She wore her hair curly and had dark brown eyes. She would always invite me to events that the NFL wives would host. I could tell neither she nor I fit in with the snotty little housewives. They would always talk down to her and overlook me because of my age. It didn't take long to figure out who the insecure wives were—or who was being cheated on.

Janice knew she didn't fit in, but I think, for the sake of being an NFL wife, she obliged. I remember her calling me one afternoon and asking me to meet her for dinner downtown. The look on her face said it all.

"What's wrong?" I asked.

She looked down at the floor and then up at me. "You remember a few weeks ago when we were at Tanya and Randall's house?"

"Yes, I remember." I was growing curious. "What about it?"

She turned her head and gazed down at the street lights from the Space Needle. SkyCity is a restaurant inside of the Space Needle that's about five hundred feet above the ground. The rotating panoramic view of downtown Seattle's lights and the people moving around below is undeniably amazing.

I put my fork down after taking a bite of my salad and grabbed her hand. The look in her eyes scared me. "What is it?" I asked again. She handed me a folded piece of paper. I slowly unfolded it and could not believe what I saw. Tanya had written a letter to Janice admitting to having a fling with Janice's husband, Donovan. This was the same lady who had invited us to her brunch a few weeks earlier. My heart ached for my friend. I didn't know what to say.

The first time I had heard of a specific instance of infidelity was when one of the ladies told us a story about her friend, whose husband had left her after she found a letter that he wrote to another woman. She left him for a month or so; when she returned home, the locks had been changed and, to her surprise, her husband had moved the other woman into her home.

I knew Janice and Donovan were having some problems, as David often talked about them, but nothing to this degree. I tried to reassure her that everything was going to be all right, but while I said it; I didn't really believe it. Besides, what did I know, and why was she telling me this? I did consider her a friend, but my God, she was almost ten years older than I was.

Just as I was about to say something else, her phone rang. It was her husband, Donovan. He was pleading with her to come home and talk things over. As we exited the elevator, she smiled and said, "I'm sorry for overreacting and putting all of this on you. We're going to be okay."

I smiled back and walked to my car.

Things with David continued to go well. I was beginning to believe I knew him, and he hadn't given me any reason to believe I was in imminent danger or treading into unknown territory. We hung out at least three to four times a month with his friends. They would smoke and do their thing while playing poker, and the wives and I would sit and gossip about what was going on in the league. Janice had swept the affair under the rug as if nothing had happened. Obviously Tanya had as well, because she continued to invite Janice to numerous outings.

I didn't see it coming, or did I? I don't even know when exactly it started going wrong, but soon into the relationship, David would tell me that he didn't like me talking to other guys. That brand of insecurity progressed, and he became more and more controlling and jealous. He didn't want me hanging out unless he knew about it and, if I did leave, he'd call me constantly, asking me when I'd be back home. I would soon see the not-so-charming side of David. I remember once when we had been out to a concert with some friends and he had had way too much to drink. His friend John jokingly asked if I needed a ride home, seeing that David was in no shape to drive. I hadn't really learned my way around yet at that point, so I'm assuming that was the reason for John asking, jokingly or not. But David didn't find it funny, and he went into a frenzy. He grabbed me by the hair to drag me to the car. I didn't want to cause a scene so I removed his hand and walked quickly to the car. Once we were both inside, he shoved my head against the passenger window, yelling that I was flirting with his friend. I forced the door open, got out of the car, and asked John to give me a ride home. I was shocked that David had behaved that way. Like I said, I did not see that coming. Or did I just turn a blind eye? It was like he snapped and became a completely different person. I didn't know what to do or what to think. I cried myself to sleep that night.

The next day he came over to see if I was okay. I am not sure if he even remembered what had happened the night before, as he had consumed quite a bit of alcohol. I could see it in his eyes that he was full of remorse. He begged and pleaded with me. I believe he made himself cry, just like actors on a movie set do. He made the promise that I think all abusers make. He said that things would be different; he would stop drinking and he promised to never hit me again. That would be a promise I knew he couldn't keep, but I made myself believe him, and things did improve—for a while.

It seemed like the honeymoon phase had started all over again. This went on for a few weeks. I was enjoying the attention. That is, until he started pressuring me to move out of my aunt Clara's home. He would say things like, "You're too old to be staying with your aunt. You have a job and no reason not to be on your own." The more he said it, the more it made sense. And besides, I was tired of my aunt Clara giving my mom weekly reports as to how I was doing. She would make her Sunday ritual calls and tell my mom the time I came home, that I was messing around with an old man (she referred to David as old), and was hanging out at parties and concerts. I loved and respected my aunt Clara dearly, but I was ready to be an adult, ready to venture out and be on my own. Besides, I now had a man to take care of me, so why should I be limited to a small room in the back of my aunt's home? That was me, trying to rationalize the biggest decision I'd ever have to make.

Several months went by and I continued with my daily routine, getting up at six a.m. to catch the number thirty-nine bus into downtown Seattle to my nice little job at the bank. David was still urging me to move out, but it just didn't feel right. Then, one evening after I got home from work, my aunt Clara called me into the living room. She was sitting on the right side of the sofa, one of her favorite spots for looking out the window. I was very apprehensive as I approached her. She had this look on her face that made me fearful. I thought that something bad had happened. I sat on the opposite end of the sofa and slowly raised my head. When I looked up, my eyes met hers. She smiled, and I was relieved for a moment.

She went on to say that she had noticed that I had been sleeping a lot after coming home from work. She beckoned me to come closer. Holding my face in her hands, she told me to tilt my head. She placed two fingers on my neck. I was so oblivious at that moment. She drew my head down into her lap and sighed, "Lord, help." I lay there wondering what she meant. Had she sensed something wrong with me to the point that she felt I needed the Lord's help? I was afraid to move. Aunt Clara stroked my head and softly whispered, "Call your mom."

I slowly sat up and looked at her. Still confused, I stuttered as I tried to get my words out. I knew my aunt Clara had been blessed with the spiritual gift of prophecy. What had she seen? After several minutes of silence between us, I mumbled, "Why do I need to call my mom?"

Aunt Clara calmly responded, "To tell her she is going to be a grandmother."

My eyes nearly popped out of their sockets. I slid to the floor and sat there in shock. It was almost like that scene from the movie *The Color Purple*, where the character Ms. Celie goes to her stepfather's funeral and stands frozen in the door of the church and says, "I can't move."

I couldn't move. A baby! Me! Pregnant! How stupid could I have been? I hadn't planned for a future with this man. I wasn't ready to be a mother. I was planning to attend law school, not have a baby. In that moment, I think I went through what felt like a thousand different emotions. "What am I going to do? I can't call my mom with this. Can I wait? I don't have to have this baby. I have options." My voice trembled. "Abortion is an option. I can't have a baby. I'm not married. This is not happening." I think I went on for what seemed like hours. Aunt Clara just rocked me in silence. She never said a word. That night I cried myself to sleep. I awakened the next morning with dark circles around my eyes, which were so swollen that I looked like I had been in the ring with heavyweight boxer Iron Mike Tyson.

I laid in bed, trying to retrace the moment the pregnancy could have happened. A light knock on my door interrupted my thoughts. It was Aunt Clara. It was early Saturday morning and she was usually out the door by that time to beat the crowd at the local thrift store. Not that day. She opted out of her Saturday routine for me.

She came in and sat on the bed and said, "You know you have to tell your mom. I am not going to do this for you." Then she looked me sternly in my eyes and with deep conviction presented the premarital sermon that I knew was coming, that had been preached repeatedly. 1 Corinthians 6:18–20:

> Flee from sexual immorality. All other sins a person commits are outside the body, but whoever sins sexually, sins against their own body. Do you not know that your bodies are temples of the Holy Spirit, who is in you, whom you have received from God? You are not your own; you were bought at a price. Therefore honor God with your bodies.

I sat there feeling like I had just received a life sentence for having committed fornication, sexual immorality. Was this the plan for my life? My mind wandered back to the little twelve-year-old girl I had been and feelings of inadequacy crept in. Had I been set up for this? Was it bound to happen? I could hear the voice of my cousin repeatedly saying, "You're a big girl now, so act like it." I had no response for my aunt Clara. For the girl that the family labeled motor mouth, I was at a loss for words.

Aunt Clara softly whispered, "It's okay and you will be okay. Now it's time to call your mom."

My heart sank. How do you tell your mom that you're pregnant, seven months after leaving home? Aunt Clara knew I wasn't ready for that, so she picked up the phone and called my mom herself. They did the usual, trading information on their shopping sprees to their local thrift stores. This went on for about twenty minutes. Then she made the announcement: "Cill has something to tell you."

I slowly reached for the telephone and tried to smile. "Hey Mom!" I made small talk about my job at the bank and how much I liked living in Seattle. Aunt Clara was sitting there looking at me, her expression almost saying, "Girl, get to the point." I looked down at the floor and softly whispered, "Mom, I'm pregnant." Despite not having had a test to confirm my pregnancy, I trusted that my aunt knew what she was talking about. It seemed like forever before my mom would respond. Surprisingly, she wasn't angry.

She said, in a very matter-of-fact tone, "You're going to have to step up!" Then she asked, "Who is the father?"

Before I could respond, Aunt Clara took the phone and answered, "Some old man across the street. He's much older than she is." I smirked at the way she described David like he was an old, gray-haired man, finding humor in her description, but only for a moment before the seriousness of the situation hit me again. My cousin was on her way to take me to the health clinic to confirm Aunt Clara's diagnosis.

We arrived at the clinic within ten minutes. Not enough time, in my book, to digest all that was going on inside my mind. There were women and children all over the place. The kids were giddy, running and sliding across the floor. Toys were strewn all over the place, while the parents went about their conversations as if this was normal behavior. I looked on and wondered how I'd raise my child if the test came back positive. Would I be like those mothers, allowing my kid to slide across the floors at the doctor's office? Just as I was processing that thought, the receptionist called my name. I rose slowly. As I approached the window, a little girl grabbed my pant leg to keep from falling. I helped her up and returned my attention to the thick packet of paperwork I was given to fill out. I completed the forms as best I could and handed them back to the receptionist.

A few moments later the nurse called me back. She started by verifying my name, then asked me to step on the scale. I sighed heavily at the number. Oh yes. I had gained a few extra pounds. After she had gotten my weight, she took my vitals—blood pressure, temperature and pulse—and handed me a plastic cup while leading me to the restroom. I was scared and hugged myself in fear of what these tests were going to confirm. I then entered a room with bright lights and the nurse instructed me to remove my clothing and put on the blue gown. I was shaking like a leaf.

Finally, Dr. Walker came in, a tall, thin, middle-aged woman with perfect teeth. She reviewed the chart notes and asked the same questions that the nurse had previously asked. After affirming the answers previously given, she began the exam. The examination was a bit invasive. All the probing seemed a bit much and was very overwhelming. I couldn't help but wonder, was all of this really needed to determine if a baby was growing inside of me? The doctor made these annoying sounds, followed by, "Oh my . . . So when did you say you had your last menstrual cycle?"

I rolled my eyes and softly whispered, "I don't know."

"Well," she said, "You're going to be a mommy in about seven months."

Suddenly my mind screamed, What is going on with the number seven? I arrived in Seattle seven months ago and now I'm going to have a child in seven months. I tried to fight back the tears that were forming, but it was too late. I felt the tears roll down the side of my face. A part of me wanted to scream but again, I could not find my voice. I was speechless. Dr. Walker instructed me to sit up and gave me a few moments to get dressed. Once she exited the room, I broke. Sobbing uncontrollably, I sat on the examination table in total disbelief.

After taking it all in, I slowly lifted myself off the table and got dressed. Dr. Walker reentered just as I was putting my shoes on and asked if I had any questions. I had a million and one questions, but I was still unable to speak. All of me prayed that it was just a dream, but I knew deep down inside that it wasn't. This would be the beginning of a new life for me. I thought—again—how could God allow this to happen to me? I was convinced I was being punished. I felt an enormous amount of shame and guilt.

God, is it too late? I would roll the question over and over in my thoughts. Then the thoughts would ramble on: Lord, I have prayed for what seems like an eternity. I was trying to do everything I knew to bring my dreams to fruition. I have had one disappointment after another. Lord, is it too late for me? Lord, please don't let me miss my destiny and please don't allow me to pray for things that are not a part of Your plan for my life. God, I only want what You believe is right for me. Let me hear Your voice telling me what You really intend for me. Was this a part of Your plan for my life, or is this my punishment? I felt hopeless. I knew I wasn't ready for a baby, especially not with David.

I walked slowly to the front of the hospital, where my cousin Greta sat reading a magazine. She'd barely noticed that I was standing there. The look on my face answered the unasked question. She knew all too well, as she had just had her first son, Tyson, a few months prior. She carefully placed the magazine on the table and headed for the exit. I followed slowly behind her. The walk from where I was to the exit felt like the green mile to the executioner's chair.

It was days after the visit to the doctor before I worked up the nerve to tell David. I was trying to convince myself that it would be okay and that, even if *I* wasn't thrilled, once I told David he would be happy. I waited for my girlfriend Stacy and her husband Jason to leave for work that morning. It was starting to rain lightly as I scurried across the street. As

I neared the front door, the dogs began to bark. David must have been out back feeding them. He came from the side of the house and playfully grabbed me from behind. I tried to smile but couldn't. We walked into the house and I sat at the kitchen table, staring out of the window. When he came back into the kitchen, he had changed into some sweats and a t-shirt. I sat nervously as he began to talk about the apartment he had found and would be moving into soon.

He started in on me about moving out of my aunt Clara's home. Little did he know, I had already decided that, if I was going to have this baby, I would have to move in with him. I got up and walked into the living room where David was sitting on the sofa watching Sports Center. I slowly sat down beside him and asked how he would feel about having a kid. He initially ignored me. "David," I said softly. "I'm pregnant."

After I told him that, he slapped my stomach so hard that I buckled to my knees. I was shocked! I would have never thought in a million years that he would hit me like that. All I could do was reach for a nonexistent wall to hold me up. While trying to recover and catch my breath, he went on a tangent, calling me all sorts of names and telling me how stupid he thought I was. I couldn't muster up a word. I felt as stupid as he said I was for not protecting myself. What was I thinking?

I slowly pulled myself together enough to make it across the street to Aunt Clara's house. As I made my way to my room, I heard a soft voice. It was Aunt Clara. She had seen me come in and knew something wasn't right. I tried talking in riddles, but Aunt Clara saw right through me. Aunt Clara had a way of knowing when something wasn't right. She was preparing dinner and the aroma of whatever she was cooking made me nauseous. I laid my head on the dining room table to avoid inhaling the aroma coming from the kitchen while she lectured me.

"You are not the first to have a baby out of wedlock and I'm sure you won't be the last. But you must understand, there are consequences. You can hold your head up and still accomplish remarkable things in your life." Was she just saying that, or did she truly believe that?

I heard what she was saying but my mind was far away. The sting of that slap to my belly was still lingering. Who the heck did he think he was? And he wanted me to move in with him? He must have been crazy! Days went by and I continued to ignore his calls. I would take an earlier bus to work or have my uncle Ray drop me off on Rainier Avenue so I could take a different bus to avoid running into David. I felt like my life was spiraling out of control. How did I get to this place? I needed time to figure out where my life was headed. I had a little life growing inside of me that was depending on me to figure it out.

Chapter 5
THE SIGNS WERE THERE

It was pouring outside. As I sat at the dining room table, contemplating whether I was ready to take this journey with David or not, I tried to weigh the pros and cons and how this could affect my future. Knock! Knock! I jumped; startled at the force being used on Aunt Clara's door. My heart dropped. Oh Lord, I thought. David must be drunk and at it again. Uncle Ray was closer than I was to the front door. He stomped his feet as he walked swiftly to the front door. He flung the door open and yelled a few expletives. But it was just my cousin Ann, soaking wet. She had come over to see how I was doing. After Ann had gone upstairs and found some of her old clothing that she had left behind at the house, she joined me at the table and we sat and talked for hours. She talked about being independent and having her own space. Ann enlightened me on the importance of having your place and being responsible for another life. That would be the defining moment for me, and I made the decision to move out. Wrong move.

I was once told a story about twin brothers who were raised by an abusive, alcoholic father. One of the brothers followed in his father's footsteps. He, too, became an abusive alcoholic. The other twin went the other way and never touched alcohol a day in his life; not even a sip. Unfortunately, my story is patterned after the brother who went on to become what he saw. Even though I promised myself that I would never allow a man to abuse me after witnessing Aunt Agnes be beaten, I, too, found myself suffering at the hand of an abusive man. At the age of nineteen, I journeyed to hell and back.

David and I moved into our new apartment two months later. It seemed like the honeymoon phase all over again, like when we first met. But although things seemed to be going well, I had a feeling of uneasiness around David. He would drink and smoke marijuana laced with cocaine all the time. Friends frequently dropped by unannounced. One evening, David had gone out with the boys and came home wasted. We argued and I told him he needed to get some help or I was going to leave. Wham! He viciously punched me in the stomach. I tried to grab ahold of the coat rack to balance myself, but it was no match for his strength. He grabbed me by my hair and attempted to kiss me. I bit his tongue. That enraged him even more. As he reached back to strike again, I grabbed the flashlight that was sitting on the arm rail counter and hit him as hard as I could. It worked. That was enough to get his drunken attention. He stumbled to the floor and began to call me all sorts of names. Names I'd never even heard before.

I went to bed that night wondering if this was a mistake. I began to entertain other options. Yes, I had options. The next morning, though, David came into the room with tears in his eyes. The look on his face said it all. Outside of the dismantled coat rack and the displaced furniture in the living room, he couldn't remember what had happened. I didn't bother to share it either. His tears moved me and I gave him an ultimatum: drinking and his friends or me. "And don't you ever put your hands on me again!" I screamed. He apologized and declared his undying love for me. I was happy—he chose me.

Choosing me did not last long. After our son was born, he started drinking again. His constant verbal abuse soon became unbearable. I stayed because, at the time, I didn't see a way out, not with a child to support. I was scared every morning of what he would do that day. I had a panic attack when he was shouting at me one day because I was just too emotionally tired of being accused of lying and cheating. I couldn't handle it anymore. I felt sick.

When he was sober, things seemed pleasant. My way of life thus turned into a vicious cycle of an on-again, off-again relationship with him. This cycle continued for about two years. My family and a few friends knew, to a certain extent, what was going on, but I had learned to hide the visible bruises and he was very good at not leaving them where they could be seen. Over the years, I filed several restraining orders against him. Every time I filed one, though, he convinced me to drop the charges. He was almost a textbook abuser. Sometimes he made promises and sometimes he made threats. No matter what I did, I could not seem to make him happy. The chicken was never seasoned properly. The bathroom was never clean enough, no matter how long I scrubbed or how much bleach I used. My hair was never pretty enough. Literally nothing that I did or said pleased him. I often felt like a hamster running aimlessly on a wheel, desperate to please him. Just once, I wanted to feel like I was enough. I longed to feel like I was worthy of his love and affection. Before long, I began to realize that I would never be enough for him—and this was not because of any fault of mine.

At that point, I was sick and tired of being sick and tired, but just not sick enough to leave. I had spent the last year or so in pure hell. When I threatened to leave, he would calm down for a week or two and the cycle would start all over again. I became numb to any- and everything he said or did. That is, until I found out I was pregnant again. I had decided months earlier that I would leave, but each time I gathered my resolve to actually do it my fears of being alone would paralyze me. Now this, and my pitiful cry returned. "Lord, what am I going to do now?"

I was petrified at the thought of having another child with David. I was so embarrassed and decided not to tell anyone. I kept it a secret until it became obvious. How could you be so reckless, I asked myself. Sitting across the table from Aunt

Clara, eyes filled with tears, I patiently waited for the sermon. I knew it was coming. She had been calling me for over a week, asking me to come by, and each time, I made an excuse as to why I couldn't. I knew she knew something was wrong, and I believe I was more afraid this time than I had been the day she told me of my first pregnancy.

She started out by saying, "I know you are in a dark place right now and you think all is lost, but I promise you it's not. God loves you. Long before you were born, He loved you. Even in your darkest and most sordid moments, God's love never fails."

I sat there speechless. I didn't believe in that moment that God loved me. I had made such a mess of my life and I wasn't deserving of anyone loving me.

Aunt Clara looked at me with eyes filled with pity and sadness. "God is not pleased with the life you're living," she said. "It's time for you to make the decision to give your life completely over to Him. You've been running in circles for a long time and getting nowhere."

"Aunt Clara, I'm pregnant again," I blurted out.

She held my hand and softy said, "I know."

"What am I supposed to do?" I glanced up at her, hoping she didn't see my shame.

"Pray," she said. "God can take your mess and turn it into a miracle if you'd just give it over to Him. You can't keep shacking up, having all these babies, and then ask God to bless you."

I knew she was right. I had been praying for God to free me from this man. I was tired, and now this. I left Aunt Clara's house determined to change my life, our life.

"You're so stupid!" David yelled. "I thought you were on the pill. How did you let this happen?" He went on for hours calling me all kinds of names and swearing like a sailor. He had been on one of his binges. I knew it may not have been the best time to share the news, but in all honesty, I had thought he knew, or at least that he should have noticed the bulge and weight gain.

But the effects of using drugs along with the alcohol distorted his vision. I sat there waiting for the punch to come, but it never did that day. David would eventually fall asleep and everything seemed calm. I sat in the room watching cartoons with my son, Josiah. He was so innocent in all of this. I asked my twenty-three-year-old self, Now what are you going to do, with two children? My heart ached. My plans to leave would be halted because of my children. I left the room so my son wouldn't see me crying. I sat out on the patio in the still darkness, feeling sorry for myself. Sorry that I messed up again. Sorry that David was in my life. Sorry for the mess I'd made. Sorry for disappointing my parents. Most of all, sorry for dishonoring God.

It was nearly daybreak. I had fallen asleep outside. I slowly opened the patio door to avoid waking David, who had passed out the night before on the couch. I tiptoed through the kitchen into my son's room. He was sleeping so peacefully. I prayed and asked God to forgive me again and again and again. My prayer life up until that point had been a consistent cry for forgiveness. I was living a life that was not pleasing to God, yet I sought His forgiveness for everything I did.

"Lord, please forgive me." I prayed. "Please help my belief and show me Your will for my life." I was depleted and absent of life, besides the one now growing inside of me. I crawled under the Ninja Turtle comforter and snuggled with my son. "I got you," I whispered in his ear, "Mommy's got you. We are going to be okay. I promise you."

Months went by and the fights continued. I was running on fumes, barely sleeping most nights, then waking up with swollen eyes. I was sick all the time.

― ―

"Good morning, Ms. Jefferson," the receptionist said as I signed in for my obstetrics appointment. Dr. Walker, my obstetrician, had called the day before and asked if I could come in for another ultrasound. She had some concerns from my appointment a few days before. I was almost seven months along and had gone in for my monthly OB-GYN appointment. That's when I'd found out I was having a girl. I was excited at the news. A mini me. I took the ultrasound photo that day and held it close to my heart. Now I'm complete, I thought. A girl and a boy. I'm done having children. I smiled to myself. This was it. As I changed out of my clothes into the hospital gown, a sense of sadness came over me. I wasn't sure, but I just felt in my spirit that something wasn't right. I had just had an ultrasound two days prior, and now Dr. Walker wanted another test. When the doctor entered the room, she had this serious look on her face. A look of concern that made me very uncomfortable, because Dr. Walker was always smiling, with words of encouragement ready to be spoken.

She looked at me with sadness in her eyes. "After you left the office the other day, I went back to look at the ultrasound again. There were a few areas in the images that concerned me and I want to repeat the procedure again."

That confirmed my suspicions that something could be wrong. As the nurse set up the table with the gel and the monitor, I asked Dr. Walker if something was wrong with the baby.

She solemnly responded, "I'm not sure yet. That's why I wanted you to come and have the sonogram done again."

I was scared. What could possibly be wrong? All sorts of thoughts started flooding my mind. I wasn't ready for nor did I think I could handle any unwelcome news. The procedure seemed to take longer this time. I laid there thinking about my life. There was another prayer of "God, rescue me. Stop punishing me," on my lips. "God, are You punishing me? I know I've been going down the wrong path for a long time, but I'm going to make it right. God, don't let anything be wrong with my little girl."

A few minutes later the nurse cleaned the gel off my belly and I got dressed. Dr. Walker came back in and sat on her stool, as close as she could to me. "Priscilla," she said softly, "I'm afraid that there might be some chromosomal abnormalities and possibly infection. There seems to be quite a bit of fluid on the baby's heart and lungs. We need to schedule another procedure to try and remove it. The procedure is invasive. However, it's necessary. I'd like to schedule it as soon as possible to give the baby a better chance of survival."

I broke down. "How did that happen?" I screamed. Dr. Walker explained the unexplainable, yet all I remember hearing was "better chance."

The procedure was scheduled for the next day. I was given a ton of paperwork to read and sign. *Amniocentesis* is what it was called. The doctor would use a monitor to guide this long, very thin needle into my stomach and the baby's heart to try and remove the fluid.

I cried during the entire procedure. "Is this hurting her?" I asked. The doctor responded no. Once the procedure was over, I laid there—once again—begging and pleading with

God to let my baby girl be all right. My prayer would fall on deaf ears. God wasn't listening to me.

Dr. Walker and Dr. Mann, the doctor who performed the procedure, came back into the room. They mounted the images on a screen and immediately I saw what looked like dark spots in certain areas of my baby girl's body.

Dr. Mann spoke first. "Ms. Jefferson, I am so sorry. We tried to remove as much of the fluid as we possibly could—but it's just too much. At this point, there is nothing more we can do. The baby has a 25 percent chance of surviving."

I sat there in a daze. I couldn't speak. I had no words, there were no tears, just a blank stare.

Dr. Walker took my hand and stroked it. "I'm so sorry," she said. "I know how hard this must be, but we must make some decisions."

Dr. Mann continued, "There is very little chance of the baby surviving, and even if she survives, she will more than likely be in a vegetative state with no sign of life. We can induce labor and take the baby now, or you can go the remainder of your term and see what happens."

What kind of options were those? I had been through enough that week and I wasn't ready. I wasn't ready to accept what the doctors were saying. I knew that God had the final say.

Chapter 6
TRAUMAS

I left the hospital that day feeling defeated. I was in a state of disbelief and I didn't want to think about what had just transpired. I was an emotional wreck. As horrific as it was, though, my breakdown was actually my breakthrough. It was an in-your-face wake-up call that forced me to realize that I was driving myself too hard, and for the wrong reasons. I finally had to say, "Enough is enough! I am done destroying myself and ruining my life!"

I had to admit to myself that my life and my children's lives were far too important and that my children needed me; God needed me to complete the work He had begun in me, if only I would submit to my calling. Though there were many obstacles yet ahead, this was the beginning of my road to recovery and true happiness.

My cousin Linda was waiting for me in the waiting room. I couldn't speak. No. I didn't want to speak. I didn't want to talk to anyone, not even God. I was angry and hurt. I felt like God had betrayed me. I felt abandoned and alone. Linda asked if I was okay and I snapped, "No, I'm not and I don't feel like talking."

She wouldn't say anything else until we reached my house. "Do you want me to come in?"

"No," I responded.

"Okay, well, call me if you need me."

I could tell she was sad for me and really wanted to be there, but I just wasn't in the right frame of mind and I needed to be alone. David had been on one of his binges and hadn't been home for two days. I was relieved when I didn't see the silver Audi parked in the driveway. My girlfriend had taken Josiah for a few days so it would be just me. Well, me and God, and I had a few bones to pick with Him. He had some explaining to do.

As I entered the house, my hands started to tremble. I put my bag down and made my way to the bedroom I shared with my son. At that point, I had not slept in the same bed as David for months. We were literally just roommates who fought all the time. My focus had shifted: I was only concerned about caring for myself and my kids and planning my getaway as soon as my daughter was born. I had saved quite a bit of money, and it was just a matter of time before I'd be free from the madness.

I lay there, still angry, and wondered how all of this had come to be. I remembered hearing my mother say, "God won't put more on you than you can bear." I couldn't believe that, because this had turned out to be way more than I could ever bear. I guess I must have drifted off to sleep because the loud ring of the telephone startled me.

It was my mom. I really didn't want to talk, but when I answered the phone, my mom was praying. After a few minutes went by, there was another voice that came on the phone. It was my aunt Clara, and then my aunt Connie joined in as well. They were praying up a storm, yet I wasn't moved. I sat there stonehearted, listening to those three powerful prayer warriors cry out to God on my behalf. But I didn't soften until my mom came back on and said, "I don't know what's going on in your life right now. You can question God all you want, but you better be prepared when He answers."

My heart sank. How did my mom know that I was angry with God and questioning Him? No one knew yet what I was facing but God. I sat quietly on the phone as they took turns prophesying to me about what God had spoken.

My aunt Connie started to sing the old hymn "Amazing Grace." Then Mom and Aunt Clara chimed in. It felt like I was back home at St. Peter Baptist Church, and the Holy Spirit filled the room. I closed my eyes and embraced that moment. I envisioned Deacon Abrams, our late minister, leading the church in prayer when I was a child. The tears began to flow;

my lower lip began to quiver uncontrollably. I began uttering words that I didn't understand. I remember running through every room in that house crying out to God in a foreign language, one only He understood. It almost felt like an out-of-body experience.

Moments later, I returned to the room, only to find the phone on the floor. When I picked it up, my mother was praying again. Chills ran up and down my spine and my body was overcome with Holy Ghost chills. John 3:8 says, "The wind blows wherever it pleases. You hear its sound, but you cannot tell where it comes from or where it is going. So it is with everyone born of the Spirit."

I knew God was speaking. I knew He used my mom and my aunts to get my attention. This was no coincidence, and their prayers were specific to what I was going through. I needed those prayers. I needed them to breathe life into a hopeless situation. I laid there thanking God for what He'd done. I heard my mom say, "In Jesus' name, amen."

I felt a sense of peace come over me. My faith in God had been revived and I realized there was a significant difference between being saved and being healed until God makes you whole. My salvation had happened in an instant, but my healing would be a lifelong process. The next morning, I called the doctor's office and told them I had decided to go ahead and have them induce my labor. I decided that whatever God's will was for her, let it be done.

Two weeks later, on June 16, 1989, at approximately 1:04 p.m., I gave birth to my baby girl, Jasmine Tiara Jefferson. It was an easy birth. She weighed in at seven pounds and four ounces. The faint cry gave me hope. Afraid of what I might see, I forced myself to look and my frightened glance showed me her fluid-filled body, surprisingly large head, and fragile limbs, shaking now in unison with her cry. The nurse wrapped her in a warm blanket after the breathing tubes had been inserted.

"I can't get a heartbeat," the nurse said. The doctor and a team of other nurses surged forward. I had already prepared myself for the *what if*. I tried to tune out the voices rattling off instructions. After several minutes, Jasmine had been stabilized. In the aftermath of the delivery, the room fell quiet. The team of doctors and nurses had vanished into thin air. Only my best friend Valerie and my nurse remained. As the nurse wheeled me out of the delivery room into recovery, I glanced at the clock: 4:46 p.m. Not even four hours from the beginning to the end.

The next morning, I forced myself out of bed. I had barely slept the night before. I was very sore and feeling sick to my stomach, but I had to see my baby girl. I pushed the breakfast tray aside and put on the fuzzy blue hospital socks the nurse gave me the night before. The first glimpse of my daughter, with the bandages and cotton dressings that surrounded her, was startling. I tried to absorb it all: the tubes, the lines, and the IVs. Her little chest vibrated from the ventilator. The nurse had removed the blanket and the only thing clinging to her was an oversized diaper. Her legs were long and desperately thin. Her body trembled and her eyes were fused shut. She had a full head of coal-black hair and a little pointy nose.

My heart ached for my baby girl. I began to cry. I couldn't save her, nothing and no one could change her outcome but God and He had already spoken. The nurse tried to offer consolation, but I rejected her and stumbled my way back to my room. Moments later a young lady came in and handed me forms to complete for Jasmine's birth certificate. "Congratulations," she smiled.

I sat in the chair near the window gazing up at the cloudy skies, with dark circles under my eyes and my hair uncombed. My mom had come up to be with me, but I didn't want her comfort. The phone rang and I ignored it. My family and friends had been calling, but I wouldn't answer. The messages piled up. They wanted to know what was going on, but I didn't care to reply. Later that evening, the doctor came in and informed me that things weren't looking good. She asked if I wanted to hold my baby girl. I twisted the tissue I had been holding all day but didn't respond. After what seemed like hours, I looked up at the doctor and nodded yes. Please bring me my daughter. I'm not sure of the significance of that tissue I had been holding on to that day, but for some reason I couldn't put it down.

The nurse rolled the incubator in and my heart skipped what seemed like a million beats. All of the tubes and monitors were more than I could handle. "Is she in pain?" I asked softly.

"Not at all," the nurse responded.

I watched her tiny little chest rise and fall with the help of the ventilator. She was wrapped in a pink blanket with white bunny rabbits all over it. My eyes were fixated on how pale she was.

"It's only a matter of time, once we remove the tubes. Are you ready?" the nurse asked.

"Yes ma'am," I replied. I could hear my mom, who was sitting and staring out the window, singing the old hymn "Amazing Grace" and praying.

Once the nurse removed all the tubes, she handed me my baby girl. She was as light as a feather. Her eyes never opened, and her small, frail body was warm to the touch. A part of me hoped for a miracle, and yet the other part wanted God to move quickly and take her. The latter would prevail. I held my baby girl and watched as she struggled to breathe; ten, maybe fifteen minutes later, she was gone. Her lips had turned blue and her body went from lukewarm to cold. I would later find out that she had been resuscitated and put back on the ventilator for me and my mom to say our final goodbyes.

I couldn't cry. I was emotionless, numb. I didn't feel anything. My mom came over and took the baby as I sat there in a state of disbelief. I could still hear her gently singing and then praying. I must have fallen asleep, because the next thing I knew, it was sunlight outside and Mom was now lying down on the sleeper chair. It was quiet as a mouse in that room. Minutes later, the chaplain came in, along with the doctor and the nurse.

"How are you feeling today?" the doctor asked. The deep baritone voice came across like thunder. Mom jumped up, startled by the sound.

"I am okay," I said.

"Good to hear," the doctor said. "All of your vitals are good, and we are going to release you to go home tomorrow. We know this has been very hard on you and your family, and we want to give you time to let this soak in, and also to make arrangements for your baby girl."

Arrangements? That was the furthest thing from my mind. I had tossed and turned all night wondering what was going on with my son. And where was David? Where had he been the past couple of days? I was so over this situation with him, and I knew it was time for change. I had to take my life back.

I began to try and put the pieces of the puzzle together as to why God allowed this to happen. Was it really a tragedy? Was this the way of escape that he had planned for me? I say escape because, had Jasmine lived, would I have tried to stay in the relationship? What if this was not a curse, as I had thought several times, but a blessing instead? I sat up in the bed and, after the chaplain read a few scriptures, we prayed. I felt a sense of peace come over me, and it felt good, refreshing, like a spiritual cleansing.

The next day, I was released from the hospital. Mom hadn't wasted any time and had already had my cousin Ann contact a local funeral home. She had made arrangements to go and look at caskets, to get things over with, and I didn't argue with her. My mom had flown all the way from Shreveport, Louisiana, to come and help me, and I would let her do just that.

It was late Tuesday evening when everything was settled. The service would be that Thursday morning at Greenwood Memorial Park, in Renton, Washington. My mom was a Godsend.

The next couple of days were grueling. The medication the doctors had put me on made me drowsy, and I slept most of the time. Mom cared for Josiah, making sure he got off to school okay and that dinner was ready when he got home. David kept his distance. He'd go to work and, once home, retreat to the bedroom. My mom didn't treat him any differently than she had before she found out about the abuse. Mom looked for the good in others, always trying to see them the way God sees them, praying for them and speaking the word of God over their lives. I yearned to be like her in that way, but I had a long way to go. My heart had hardened toward David, and I longed for the day I'd be rid of him. My plan to escape the year before had been thwarted when I found out I was pregnant with Jasmine, but since God had seen fit to take her, I was convinced that it was time.

After we got Josiah off to school on Wednesday, Mom and I headed to the funeral home. I had to dress my baby for her burial the next day. I was feeling okay, and I told my mom I was okay to dress her. But then I saw her small, lifeless body lying on a cold table, next to the white casket with light pink lining. She was just lying there, on a little blanket, with nothing on. I lost it! I guess, in my mind, I had thought they would at least have something on her.

The mortician grabbed me before I hit the floor and sat me in a nearby chair. I was mortified, but I had no strength. The tears began to flow. I wept like a baby—not for her, but for me. I was broken beyond repair at that moment. Broken in a way that only God could put back together. My mom came over and sat next to me; she cradled me in her arms until my tears subsided. The lights were dim and it was a bit chilly in the room. My mom began to pray and call on the name of Jesus. I could feel the presence of the Holy Spirit in the room. I felt the chills, I felt the release, I felt revived.

The gentleman that had kept me from falling earlier had tears in his eyes. He said, "I've never heard anyone pray like you, ma'am. God bless you." He walked toward the door and looked back. "Take all the time you need. I understand what you're going through."

Mom looked at him and said, "Thank you." I was still unable to move, so my mom did the honors of dressing her grandbaby. She had purchased her a comb and brush set, a little white bunny, and a tiny bracelet with an engraved cross that read "Rest In Peace, Our Little Angel."

After about an hour or so she was perfect. She looked like a little doll. Mom had put lotion on her coal-black hair to lay it down. Then she had placed a white headband with a big pink bow on her head. Yes, she was indeed an angel who had received her wings. My heart was happy. I smiled, and, at that moment, I was ready to let go. I would never have made it through that time without my mom and her prayer that opened my heart to receive some clarity on why God had taken my baby.

The day that I laid my baby girl to rest, I awakened to the smell of crisp bacon and the roaring sounds of the late James Cleveland singing "I don't feel no ways tired." Mom had it blasting as she puttered around in the kitchen. I washed up and joined her and my son for breakfast. Mom called out to David to join us. Once he was seated, Mom grabbed his hand and looked at me to join hands with them; I obliged. Mom began to fervently pray the Lord's Prayer before ushering us into her pleas with God. I wasn't moved. As a matter of fact, I was angry. Angry that I had to pretend that everything was okay when it wasn't. Angry that it was the day I had to say goodbye to the daughter I had longed for, although not with David. Nonetheless, I was angry.

Mom finished praying and we sat and ate in silence until the ringing of the phone broke it. I jumped up from the table and answered.

"Good morning," Aunt Clara said. "Are you ready?"

"We will be leaving in an hour," I replied.

"Okay, I'll see you soon," she said before hanging up.

As I walked back to the dining room table, I could feel David's eyes piercing right through me. I looked at him with such disdain. "Lord, help me to not hate this man," I mumbled underneath my breath. I knew I was better than that. I knew that, after I buried my baby, I would have to take drastic measures to get away from David. I could no longer live like that.

We drove separate cars to the graveside service. It was a small memorial with just family. The minister read a scripture and a prayer and that was it. My son read a poem and placed it on her casket. Mom said a prayer as we placed pink roses on her small white casket. Then Aunt Clara dismissed us with a song and a prayer. All was well that day.

A few weeks after I had buried my daughter, as I was preparing dinner, something inside of me started to boil almost as vigorously as the water for the pasta I was cooking, the spaghetti that was David's favorite. I knew something was off with him, more off than usual. I didn't know what was going on, but I was on high alert and ready to do battle that night if I needed to. He walked into the kitchen, brushing past me quickly, and headed toward the refrigerator. He grabbed a beer and then went back into the living room and plopped down on the couch. That poor couch had become forever stamped with the imprint of his backside because he spent so much time there. Suddenly, I saw something out of the corner of my eye. It was his full, unopened beer can, flying full speed toward my head. Thank God, I saw it in time to duck.

Surely I would have been unconscious for God knows how long had I not been so fortunate and quick. Before I could stop to think about what had happened, I grabbed the butcher knife out of its wooden block and flung it with all my might at him. Dang it, I thought. I had missed and it landed in one of our plants instead. I have got to work on my aim, I decided. However, if at first you don't succeed, you must always try, try again! Try again I did! I picked up the boiling pot of pasta and ran toward him. When he saw what I was doing, he raced into the next room where our infant son was sleeping, picking and holding him up in front of his face, using him as a human shield. What a coward! I had never been more disgusted with him. Every ounce of my body hated every ounce of him in that very moment. So, I allowed the situation to de-escalate. I gathered my baby boy and left.

As I drove away, I was a little afraid of what my future looked like, but not as scared as I had been during the last couple of years that I had spent on that merry-go-round. The eggshells I had been walking on were gone and no longer did I have to quiet my son when he cried. I was determined, and with the Lord on my side I was going to turn my life around.

I spent a month or so with my godmother, who also lived in Seattle, trying to build a life for my son and myself. I tormented myself daily with thoughts of David finding me. I was afraid of every shadow that followed me, even my own. It took roughly seven months before I was finally settled and felt confident enough to move out on my own. The transition was inevitable; and, while it was unclear to me how all of it was going to work out, I knew I had to trust God.

Chapter 7
KEEP YOUR FRIENDS CLOSE AND YOUR ENEMIES CLOSER

My life was good. I had started attending church services regularly with my aunt Clara. It felt good. I began to pray more, asking for God to show me His plans for my life. I had learned that you did not make major moves in your life just because things were uncomfortable, and I realized God had placed me in a difficult situation to grow my character. To grow my faith in Him. He allowed me to go through a dry season so that I could see His hand move in my life. Over many months, I sought the Lord in prayer about my life. I concluded that I had acted on my own in making decisions that weren't in line with His will for my life.

And so, I waited for the Lord to guide my steps. In the meantime, I went about my life, working as if working unto the Lord. Enjoying the fruits of my labor. Enjoying the freedom and peace of mind. Loving and caring for the most important person in my life, my son. He seemed so happy. I showered him with the best that life could offer. Just the two of us, I would always sing to him. I was comfortable; too comfortable. I let my guard down and confided in an old friend, Rosie, about my new life. I'd seen her at the mall and she and I had had lunch. She had told me that it had been years since she'd seen David and that his friend Don had told her about the abuse I suffered.

Not having anyone to really talk to about what had happened, I fell for it. We exchanged numbers and began to chat almost daily. I invited her to my home several times. That would turn out to be one of the worst mistakes of my life. Suddenly, I realized weeks had gone by with no word from Rosie. I'd call her and she wouldn't return my calls. After about a month or so I gave up. It was like she just disappeared. Well, she did, and I would soon find out why.

It was just an ordinary day. I'd finished cleaning and preparing our clothes for church the next day. It was cloudy and raining outside. I was sitting on a large green and orange beanbag chair watching Teenage Mutant Ninja Turtles with my son. This was our ritual.

Knock! Knock! Knock! Ding dong! Ding dong! I slowly got up from the floor. I wasn't expecting any company, and normally my family and friends didn't stop by without calling first. I looked through the peep hole and saw, to my surprise, that it was David. I nearly fainted. How did he find out where I lived? Then it hit me. Rosie! I sighed. I eased away from the door, hoping he couldn't see my movement from the other side. I muted the television and closed the blinds to the patio. My son had fallen asleep, which made it easier for me to pretend no one was home. Bang! Bang! Bang! He was pounding on my door. I quickly grabbed my son and took him to his room, closing the door so he wouldn't be disturbed.

"I know you're in there. I can see your car parked out front!" he yelled. "I just want to see my son. I just want to tell you I am sorry." He begged and pleaded from the other side of the door, making all sorts of promises about how he had changed. Did he really think that I was going to believe that he had been attending church and anger management classes? He poured on the charm and laid out the strategic plan he had come up with for how he was going to make our life so much better. He almost had me convinced, but God.

David begged and pleaded for what seemed like hours. Then there was complete silence. I waited a few minutes before I inched my way to the door. I looked through the peep hole. The coast was clear. Fear began to creep in. He knew where we lived. Was I going to have to move again? Lord, my soul cried, I can't do this anymore.

I wouldn't sleep that night. I sat in the darkness thinking of all the abuse I had endured at the hands of my son's father. The one thing that I realized is that suffering abuse makes you feel like your abuser is omnipresent. This was all part of his twisted plan to completely control and manipulate my life. He knew that if he hurt me often enough, I would develop a serious fear of him. Mission accomplished. I felt he would always be watching and always know what I was doing, because he knew where we lived. This led to months of constant, harassing threats.

One morning, I was heading out for work and, when I went to unlock my car door, my key wouldn't go in the lock. It was freezing outside. "Dang it!" I yelled. "Not today." Surely it wasn't cold enough for ice to form in the lock on my car door. Wham! A hard punch landed against my head. My body folded across the hood of my car. Unable to catch my balance, I slid to the ground. Before I knew it, David was attacking me. I struggled until I could break free of his grip around my neck. A neighbor yelled and David ran away before the police reached the scene.

Another time I was coming home from work and I noticed that the door was slightly ajar. I quickly ran to a neighbor's home and called the police. We learned that David had broken in and ransacked our home. He had placed a lot of our clothes in the bathtub and ruined them by filling it with water, condiments, and other food items. David became an expert at finding the perfect time to attack me. He was obsessive. He knew when I would be alone and he knew how to act quickly before the police were called. We tried to get away from him by moving to a new place, but then I fell into the same trap as the last time. Feeling lonely, I had reconnected with someone else who I thought was my friend—who then turned around and gave David my new address. The stalking and harassment resumed.

It was during this time that I realized, in my process of emerging from being broken into healing and wholeness, that I had developed the mentality of a victim. In my understanding, I had believed that, if I had only tried harder, my abuser would have loved me instead of hurting me emotionally, physically, spiritually, or sexually. I had believed that the success of my relationship with David had been totally up to me.

Not understanding that boundaries needed to be established, I had believed that love was something that I could earn by being who he wanted me to be, and I had spent my energy trying to figure out who that was and what he wanted me to do. I had never considered my own feelings, hopes, and dreams, or the idea that I could fulfill them. I had been expecting them to be fulfilled by David. I had become a self-made victim, thinking I couldn't make any changes unless he said so.

Being spiritually grounded and surrounding myself with positive-thinking individuals was something that came in handy and made a positive difference *after* I sorted out the foundation of the problem. When I understood my victim-based mentality in this new way, I could sort things out from a different perspective, which was a big key to overcoming the pain and not allowing my fear to paralyze me.

One night, as I was lying in bed and thinking about the situation with David, I decided that I had to accept my reality and expose my truth, one snapshot at a time. The reality was that I needed God. I needed His hand of protection over me and my son. Praying was my only option. I crawled out of bed and petitioned God:

In this manner, therefore, pray:

Our Father in heaven,
Hallowed be Your name.
Your kingdom come.
Your will be done
On earth as it is in heaven.
Give us this day our daily bread.
And forgive us our debts,
As we forgive our debtors.
And do not lead us into temptation,
But deliver us from the evil one.
For Yours is the kingdom and the power and the glory forever. Amen.

Matthew 6:9–13

I laid there at the side of my bed, prostrate before the Lord. In the stillness of the dark, just me and God. Hoping that God had heard my simple prayer. My mind wandering.

"Mommy, I'm hungry," a little voice whispered as he pushed at my back.

I rolled over on the plush carpet beneath me and looked up into the eyes of my son. He'd slept through the night. Apparently, I had fallen asleep on the floor. I got up, washed my face, and brushed my teeth. Josiah had settled in the living room on his Ninja Turtles beanbag, waiting patiently for me to turn on his favorite cartoons and prepare his favorite pancakes. I obliged.

As I sat and watched him eat, I started to dwell on my so-called friend's betrayal. Ring! Ring! The phone startled me. I hesitated for a moment. Had David gotten my new phone number too? I slowly lifted the receiver to my ear and waited for the caller to say something.

"Hello!" my mom shouted.

"Oh, hey Mom," I happily replied. I started catching up with her, which included complaining about the latest issue involving David.

"You just have to pray for that man," Mom suggested.

"Mom, I'm tired," I replied. "I'm tired of dealing with people. He would never have known where I was if I had not been so desperate to fill the emptiness, or if I had not been so lonely and trusted the wrong person." I went on for a while, whining and crying.

"Stop it!" my mom finally yelled. "Don't you let the devil steal your joy. You keep your head up and keep doing what you know you need to do."

I gave in. "Yes, ma'am."

We then started laughing about me crying. I loved my mommy. She kept it real and never tried to sugarcoat things. Mom called it as she saw it.

After I finished talking with my mom and hung up the phone, I realized that it was mid-morning and I still hadn't decided what my son and I would do that day. When I asked Josiah, he jumped up and down. "Movie, Mommy. Let's go have popcorn and movie." I looked up the next movie time and told my son he had a date. I had just enough time to finish up a few more chores before we left, as the movie didn't start until around four. But then the peace of the moment was broken.

"Mommy, Mommy!" Josiah screamed in his tiny little gruff voice from his seat at the dining room table. "Daddy is outside by your car!" I rushed to get dressed, frantic to get to my son as I listened to him move closer to the door.

"Mommy, Mommy, come see, my daddy is outside and he's trying to get in our car!" my son yelled as he stood staring out the patio door.

I scurried to get my jeans on, tripping on one leg as I finally made it to the living room. I pulled open the blinds that covered the patio door and, sure enough, there was David, trying to get the hood of my car up. I fumbled for the phone while keeping my eyes on him. As he fiddled with the latch on the hood of the car, a neighbor came out of his house across the street and, apparently, startled him. When he turned away from Mr. Johnson, David's eyes met mine. He had the crazed look of a madman. When he saw I had the phone in my hand, he gave the thumbs-up sign and quickly disappeared.

That disappearance made our lives good again. We later learned that he had been sentenced to ninety days in jail for breaking into our apartment months prior. For the next four months, we were able to return to a sense of normalcy. But David was eventually released from jail, and he had become obsessed with making my life miserable. I later learned from the neighbors that he had been casing the area for weeks before he acted. He had been monitoring our every move, looking for the perfect opportunity. Crazy as a fox wouldn't define this type of behavior. This time, when I saw him again messing around with my car, I quickly grabbed the phone and called 911, making sure he could see me calling.

"911. What's your emergency?" The operator asked.

"My son's father was outside of my apartment. He's not supposed to be here. I have a restraining order."

"What is he doing?" she asked.

"He was messing around under the hood of my car."

"Where is he now?" she asked sternly.

"I don't know, he ran when he saw me with the telephone in my hand."

"What is your son's father's name?"

"David Higgins," I answered in a panic.

"Okay. We have an officer on the way. Stay inside and wait."

I placed the phone down and walked over to the patio door to make sure he had disappeared. It seemed like only moments later that the police arrived. They took the report as they had done many times before. Officer Maria Davis (Lord, I will never forget that name) had gone through previous call logs and reviewed the number of times the police had been called to my home several months ago. She hugged me and confidently said, "We are going to catch this guy. You will never be free to live if he's on the streets."

I sobbed, not so much for me but for my son. He didn't deserve this. Officer Davis allowed me to cry on her shoulder. She assured me it was going to be okay. I believed her. As the police were leaving, Officer Davis came back and asked if I had any protection. Funny that she'd asked, because my cousin Sherry had just given me a can of mace. She had been concerned about my safety and it was legal to carry. I nodded a firm yes to Officer Davis. She hugged me and reinforced her position: they were going to get him.

I felt better. So much so that I decided to give my son a treat and take him to the movies. "Put your shoes on." I said to Josiah.

"Mommy, are we going to the movies?"

"Yes, son," I replied.

I grabbed my jacket and keys and we headed for the door and then I stopped dead in my tracks.

A little voice inside my head said, Don't forget your mace!

I walked back into the kitchen and grabbed the mace off the counter. Son in tow, I headed once again for the door. I turned the doorknob slowly—but as I opened the door, to my surprise there was David! My heart dropped. He shoved me back into the apartment and started making demands. I stood there, stunned, wondering: Where did this fool come from? How did he avoid all those cops that were outside moments ago?

I pulled myself together and told my son to go to his room. He stood there, frozen. "Son," I screamed. "GO TO YOUR ROOM!"

David was pacing and calling me all sorts of names. "This is what you're going to do," he said. "I'm going to lie down in the back seat of your car and you're going to take me to the North End."

"I'm not taking you anywhere," I yelled. "It's me or you today! I'm not afraid of you!"

He rushed toward me and I stumbled back into the kitchen. I quickly remembered I had the mace in my pocket, pulled it out, and began to spray him. That was no match for that crazed maniac, though. His eyes pierced through the haze caused by the mace into mine. I wouldn't back down. He grabbed a flowerpot that was sitting on the entrance table and flung it at me before charging again, this time backing me into the corner of the kitchen where the knife block was.

I grabbed the first knife I could get and began swinging. I couldn't see because of the mace, but suddenly I heard a scream and then nothing. Silence. I stumbled to the kitchen sink to wash my eyes when I heard the sirens. David was nowhere to be found. I heard the police reenter the house and watched the officers rush past me further into the house. Where were they going? I thought. I'm in here. Moments later, Officer Davis emerged from my son's room, holding him tightly. She rushed him outside to a waiting ambulance. I began to cry; eyes burning from the mace and barely able to see, I made my way outside.

While the paramedics were tending to my son, Officer Davis walked me over to another ambulance. By now a crowd had gathered. Officer Davis informed me that my son had dialed 911 and dropped the phone. She had heard the call and knew the address was mine.

"What happened?" Officer Davis asked. There was blood all over the sleeve of my shirt. As the paramedics rolled my sleeves up, there were several cuts on my arm that I hadn't noticed getting.

"This could have been a lot worse," one of the paramedics commented.

"Did anyone else get injured?" an officer asked. "There's too much blood in the house and on the sidewalk, and the extent of your wounds doesn't add up."

Before I could answer, Officer Davis was being summoned on her radio. "Suspect in custody! Suspect in custody. Black male, six feet, apprehended at suspect's home under bed. Need an ambulance."

Oh Lord, did he do something stupid to get shot? Why did they need an ambulance? My mind was racing. I paused and took a deep breath before asking for my son. Officer Davis said he was fine and beckoned the paramedic to bring him to me. He was just fine. Thank God! That was all that mattered—my son was well. After the paramedics bandaged up my cuts and we were cleared, Officer Davis informed us that we could not sleep in the apartment that night. The fire department had warned against it. Too much mace had been sprayed and, for health reasons, we needed to let it air out.

Another officer volunteered to keep an eye on Josiah while I packed some clothes. I slowly walked toward the front door. Fighting back the tears, I silently thanked God for keeping me and my son safe. "Thank you, God," I cried. "Thank you!"

We stayed at my cousin Sherry's house for the weekend. I replayed the events repeatedly in my mind. Remember, I kept telling myself, God did not bring this on me. However, He allowed it. He allowed it because He knew I would make it through this. I knew that God had already determined when and how I would come out of this despair. Unknown to me at the time, however, I still had a few more years of suffering to go. Why? Because I was not sincerely ready to start the healing process. I had not had enough. There would be more yet for me to learn.

"For sin, seizing the opportunity afforded by the commandment, deceived me, and through the commandment put me to death. So then, the law is holy, and the commandment is holy, righteous and good." Romans 7:11–12 (NIV)

"Lord, You are the God of my desert and all my dry places. I am stuck here again in this wilderness, helpless and hopeless in this desolate place. I've been here many times before, feeling trapped between where I am and where I want to be. Like the children of Israel, I am wandering and wondering, will I ever get out of here? Is there a place beyond all this fear and pain?

"God, it's not that I can't put one foot in front of the other; it's that I want to be where I am not. I need the God of fire by night and cloud by day. I need directions from the Creator of the stars. I believe there is a promised land before me; a place of healing, a place of peace, a place of provision. Lord, I long for the days of walking in the wilderness to soon come to an end. I want to go forward with you. Lord, lead me home."

Chapter 8
ANGER

Several months went by and I had not received any information from the courts regarding David's sentencing. I had no clue what he'd been charged with. All I knew was that, for months after the last arrest, I walked around in fear. Even with my new love interest Michael being there for us, I was still fearful that David would somehow come back and finish what he had started. Even behind bars, his harassing threats did not cease.

It was an otherwise ordinary day when the sound of the phone startled me. I jumped up and answered at the same time the answering machine came on. I allowed the recording to finish before I yelled, "Hello! Hello?"

"Hey, you ——!" the voice screamed from the other end of the receiver. It was David. "You can't get away from me. I got something for you as soon as I get out of here!"

My heart skipped several beats as I slammed the phone down. How in the world did he get my number? How was he able to make outgoing calls from jail? I looked at the caller

ID, only to find the number he was calling from had been blocked.

I would continue to receive calls two to three times a day from blocked numbers, and I would never answer them. Then, one day, a call came in from a regular phone number. I knew David hadn't been released so I answered; again, the answering machine had beaten me to the punch.

"Hello," I said with a smile.

"Where is my son? I want to talk to my son, you ——."

I yelled back this time. "You will never talk to my son, and whoever this low-down, dirty dog is that's interceding on your behalf and calling my home, I'm sending this number to the police." The call dropped immediately. I raced to the dining room to see if the answering machine had recorded the conversation; it had.

I went into the living room to catch my breath. I was scared and pacing the floor, trying to figure out my next move. I scrolled through my phone and dialed the number of the prosecutor's office that was handling David's case. There was no answer, so I left an urgent message. A few hours later, the prosecuting attorney's paralegal called me back.

"Ms. Priscilla, we received your message, and the lead prosecutor wants to know if you have saved the messages."

"Yes, I have them," I replied.

"Can you bring them downtown tomorrow morning? The judge would like to hear them in his chambers."

Early the next morning, I got my baby boy dressed and we made our way downtown to the King County Superior Courthouse. I asked the Lord to please let this be the last time I had to make that trip because of David's foolishness. I was sick and tired of being sick and tired of him. A part of me was becoming angry and unafraid. I felt a sense of power starting to build up in me. Power to take charge and take my life back, not for my sake but for the sake of my son.

As I approached security with the medium-sized backpack that housed my answering machine and the evidence on it, I smiled and greeted the guard with a warm and pleasant, "Good morning!"

"Good morning to you," he replied.

I laid my handbag on the belt and proceeded to walk through. After I gathered my purse and backpack, we hopped on the elevator and headed to courtroom fifty-six. The court clerk checked me in, and it wasn't long before my son and I were being ushered into Judge Rufus Simms's chambers. He was a middle-aged, gray-haired man with ocean-blue eyes. The prosecutor, a tall, lanky young man, introduced himself as the public defender. He still gets the opportunity to be represented. This is crazy, I thought to myself as I rolled my eyes.

The judge had a file in front of him and I could clearly see it was David's. There was a photo of David with his prison ID number, 9991428009. It gave me chills. The bailiff swore me in and asked for the evidence and I handed him the backpack. He carefully removed it and plugged it into the wall. The red light came on and the machine beeped. That was the indication that there were messages. The judge nodded his head and the bailiff pressed play.

"Hey, you no good ——. You can't get away from me. I got something for you as soon as I get out of here." He played the next message, and the next, and so on. I could tell by the look on the judge's face that he was infuriated. He waved his hand to the bailiff to stop the tape.

"That's enough," he said.

The prosecutor addressed the judge and then David's attorney spoke: "Clearly, your honor, there has been some sort of mistake. This is not my client's voice on the recorder."

My eyes were about to jump out of my head. "Your honor, this is ridiculous. This is Mr. Higgins, and no disrespect to his attorney, but he is lying."

The judge looked at me and nodded his head. "The court undeniably believes this is indeed Mr. Higgins on these recordings and hereby revokes all phone privileges until sentencing."

"Thank you, Jesus," I silently whispered.

After the judge dismissed us from his chambers, I pulled the prosecutor aside and asked why David hadn't been charged or had a hearing yet. He explained, "The court system is so backed up right now. But you can rest assured, he's not getting out anytime soon. With what we have on him and the additional threat charges, he's looking at up to five years."

I was furious. He could have killed me and my son, and that's all the time he could possibly get? The prosecutor explained, "We charged him with the most serious crimes we could—class C second degree domestic violence, malicious mischief, and felony harassment."

As disheartening as it was, I felt a sense of relief. I supposed that five years of peace was better than a lifetime of harassment. I left the courthouse feeling a little justified.

When I got home, I picked up the phone to call my mom and let her know what had happened. She sighed with relief and then began to pray. I vaguely remember her asking God to give me a heart to forgive David and to remove any hatred that I may have had in my heart toward him. I didn't know what to say or how to respond.

"Why are you praying for me to forgive David?" I asked.

"Because I could hear excitement in your voice when you told me of his fate. Yes, he hurt you. Yes, he did wrong and deserves to be punished, but he is still one of God's children."

I stared at the phone in disbelief. I was speechless. I could feel anger rising in my spirit as my mother continued to speak. As soon the opportunity presented itself for me to interject, I took it. "Mom, I have to make a few more calls, I will call you later. I love you," I said quickly, and without waiting for a response, I hung up.

I love and respect my mom and would never in a million years argue a point with her about God and what He gives her to share with me, but forgiveness was more than I could handle in that moment. I sat on the floor staring at the phone. "Lord," I cried out. "I don't want to forgive David, and even if I did, I don't know how to. I'm angry and bitter and need You to help me. With all the hell he's put me and my son through, five years is nothing. I have to rebuild and relocate just to feel at peace. This isn't fair. God, what's the plan, here? What is this? God! Say something!"

I was angry at God, but I was also afraid that God was angry with me. He felt unapproachable. On top of everything that had transpired in the past few months, I felt like not even God was there. And that only heightened my pain. Although it felt like I didn't have much faith, faith was all I had in that moment. I knew deep down in my heart that although I was angry with God, He would eventually answer.

I understood (and understand) that faith doesn't always look like quick answers and miracles, or parades of victory down the street. Sometimes, faith looks like trusting God despite what you see, how you feel, and what you think you know. Showing up for the battle and being ready to go to war. Abiding in the word of God when it feels like an empty and futile routine. Still lifting your hands in praise and worship, even with tears running down your face. Talking to God, because I knew (and know) deep down, He really was still there. I had to press toward forgiving David in that moment. That took crazy faith and was, perhaps, the most tenacious act of faith I've ever had to experience. When you have nothing left, you still don't let go of the rope, because you know it's your lifeline.

"For I know the plans I have for you," declares the Lord, "plans to prosper you and not to harm you, plans to give you hope and a future." Jeremiah 29:11 (NIV)

God had a plan. I know it may sound cliché for most Christians, but for some reason, this simple reality brought me such peace. There really was a plan. God was not doing damage control. God is sovereign, and if He allowed all of this to happen, certainly He had a plan to use it for my good. Period. I leapt to my feet and sprang into action. God has a plan; I repeated it over and over again. And so did I.

Chapter 9
LOVE AT FIRST SIGHT

Love at first sight is often said to be overrated. Many people find it difficult to believe in the spontaneity and magic of it—and I now see why. I met Michael at a nightclub. He was tall and handsome and had a smile that would make you give him your life savings. We danced and talked, then danced and talked some more. By the end of the night I felt like Cinderella. I had met my prince charming—or had I?

Michael was a southern breed from New Orleans, Louisiana. He had joined the US Navy three years prior and, as fate would have it, eventually landed in Washington. Michael would woo me with all the things I thought I wanted. He showered me with gifts. He would sit quietly, often stroking my back, and listen to me as I poured out my heart about all the abuse and pain David had inflicted. He took it all in and assured me he was not David and would never put his hands on me. He kept that promise. He never laid a hand on me.

It was March 1990. Michael had just returned from a six-month deployment in the Philippines. It had been six long months and I was so happy to see him. During that time, I had been promoted from a teller to an account manager at the bank. I had moved into my own apartment and my son seemed to be adapting well. We were on our way to having a normal life. Michael worked in Bremerton, Washington, during the week and would visit on the weekends. He spent a lot of time with Josiah, taking him to the park, reading to him, and teaching him how to ride his tricycle. This warmed my heart, as we had not had any contact with David for months. It felt good. I was finally free and had a fresh start.

Things were going well with Michael and me. He had decided not to reenlist in the Navy and to make a life with me and my son in Washington. No more deploying for months at a time and enduring long commutes to work. Things were moving fast, and almost before I knew it, Michael had practically moved in.

He had kept his word and not reenlisted in the navy. After a month or so Michael went to work for the US Postal Service. Life was good. We were in a good place and headed in the right direction. Nearly three months after celebrating our first holiday together, I began to have serious bouts of anxiety. I couldn't sleep and everything I ate made me sick. At work one day, I realized I had been in this position before. I sighed, took an early lunch, and headed to the nearest pharmacy to grab a pregnancy test kit with two tests. I was ready for this, but Michael had already said he didn't want kids.

I hurried back to work and decided to go to the ladies' room on a different floor than mine. I tore the wrapper off quickly and administered the test. One line meant negative, two lines meant positive. As the urine saturated the stick, two hot pink lines immediately appeared. I felt nauseated. I tried to throw up, but nothing came up.

I waited a few moments before I attempted the second test. It was hard because I had already emptied my bladder, but somehow, I mustered up enough to saturate the second stick—two more hot pink lines appeared. I was in shock. I was on the pill; even though I sometimes forgot, it should not have been often enough for this to happen. My life was going good; having another baby was the last thing on my mind. I contemplated how I was going to tell Michael. The remainder of my work day seemed to drag along and I was very unproductive.

In every life, a little rain must fall. We all experience moments when the unexpected happens, and it hits us like a ton of bricks. On the drive home, I kept trying to trace my steps. When? Why? What am I doing wrong? God, why is this happening?

Just as quickly as I asked, He answered: *"My word does not change. Sex outside of my will, marriage, is immoral.*

"When you disregard My plan for marriage, engaging in sexual activities always results in these kinds of spiritual or physical consequences: grieving the Holy Spirit, guilt, shame, regret, loss

of respect for yourself, poor role modeling, pain for your future spouse, and abortion. Sex for the physical pleasure of it damages your spirituality and pulls you away from fellowship with Me."

Tears began to flow. I knew I was wrong. I knew I had broken the very promise I had made to abstain from all sexual immorality until I married. Then I tried to manipulate the situation: But God, we plan on getting married. I'm certain that made God laugh uncontrollably. I had jokes. All jokes aside, I pulled into my parking space and noticed Michael's truck was parked in his respective spot. He knew as soon as I walked in that something was wrong. The bloodshot, puffy red eyes surely gave it away.

"Babe," he said softly. "What's wrong?"

"I'm pregnant!" I blurted out, sobbing in shame.

Michael sighed and pushed me away. That represented all he wanted to say but could not put into words. Then he grabbed me and pulled me close to him. Neither of us wanted to face reality just yet. In fact, we spent the rest of the day trying to avoid any definitive action.

Fearing the consequences of having another child, we chose the bliss of ignorance. The next morning, though, I made an appointment to confirm what I already knew. Dr. Lyles concurred: "Congratulations! You're going to have a Christmas baby!" His words fell on unappreciative ears. Neither Michael nor I said a word. I got dressed and waited for the nurse's instructions and my next appointment date.

I already knew what Michael was thinking and I wasn't going down that road with him again, not with how I felt about the last time . . .

— —

"You're late again," Michael had said. It had only been two months into our relationship, but the honeymoon phase was over. In fact, it had never really existed. I had gotten pregnant early in the relationship. I didn't want to have the baby and neither did Michael. He accompanied me to the abortion clinic. I sat in the waiting area, terrified someone would recognize me. But I just wanted to make the pregnancy go away. After I was given a pregnancy test, Michael and I were taken to a private office for a counseling session. There the counselor told me what I desperately wanted to hear.

"Although the test is positive, you shouldn't consider yourself pregnant," she explained. "It's just cells dividing, and we can take care of the problem quickly and you'll never have to worry or think about it again."

Deep sigh. I agreed to go ahead with the procedure. I signed the papers without having to discuss them with Michael. He had already made his feelings known the week before. After the signing, I was whisked away for the procedure.

The doctor administered the anesthesia and I drifted off to sleep, glad the horrible ordeal would soon be over. But when I awakened in the recovery room, instead of feeling relieved, I was besieged by a growing sense of guilt and fear of the consequences. It felt as if the doctor had aborted a part of my heart along with my baby.

I broke down; unable to control my tears, I cried hysterically. Michael heard me and charged into the recovery room, picking me up off the recovery table and carrying me to the car. I cried all the way home, and didn't stop crying for days.

Michael didn't understand and tried everything he could to help me get it together. I was depressed and I wanted to talk about what we'd done, but Michael didn't.

Weeks went by. I couldn't focus at work. My coworkers noticed. My clients noticed. I needed time off. My boss agreed.

I took a week's vacation and stayed in the apartment, feeling as if I were covered in a shroud of death. I hovered over my son. I became even more protective of him.

Weeks later, Michael thought he had an answer to my grief: "Let's get married. I know you want to be married and I'm ready to do right by you and Josiah. Priscilla, will you marry me?"

My heart melted. For the first time in months, I felt happy. "Yes, I'll marry you!" I squealed as I leapt into his arms.

Marrying the man of my dreams will make everything better, I said to myself. I was excited and ready to plan my wedding. We started looking for a house and really planning our future together. Within months, we were moving into our new home. It was amazing. At the age of twenty-six, I finally had a home of my own, a two-story, four-bedroom, three-bath house with a huge family room. It featured a large backyard with a deck and a beautiful gazebo. I was happy. The day we closed on the house, I had already scheduled an interior decorator to come measure for the custom drapes I wanted. I love the color white and opted to go with off-white drapes and furniture. I purchased a plane ticket for my mom to come and put her magical touch on the house. Everything was falling into place. Or was it? Had I become caught up in the material things that afforded me a good life with Michael, or was I trying to make something out of nothing?

Remembering the despair I felt before, I looked across the room at Michael and refused to look away. He broke the stare first. I knew then I'd won. "I'm not having another abortion," I said softly.

He looked at me and said, "I know."

We left the doctor's office and drove all the way home in silence. After Michael got me settled, he left. He'd be gone for hours. When he got back, he didn't want to discuss our future or the baby. We fought constantly throughout the rest of our engagement. I was quick to anger, even over trivial things.

Everything came to a head when I confronted Michael the morning after our wedding dinner fiasco. The whole event had made me feel like Michael would always choose to stick up for his old family, specifically his sister, and not his wife. I called off the engagement and the wedding.

"I can't do this. You act like you don't care that I'm hurting. You're insensitive and certainly haven't been treating me as if you love me," I told him.

"We need premarital counseling," Michael agreed.

We scheduled an appointment with a Christian counselor and poured out our hearts to him. It took twenty minutes before the counselor said, "I can't help you. Both of you have some emotional issues that you need to resolve before you even think about getting married."

He referred us to another counselor. Things got worse. We couldn't even have a discussion without getting into an argument.

After the fourth visit with the counselor, I was overwhelmed by despair. This was a hopeless situation. No one seemed to be able to help us—not even God. My prayers for restoring our relationship seemed to go unanswered and I became weary in my faith.

I wanted to marry Michael, but this was too much. I was an emotional wreck and knew the stress wasn't good for the baby. I had to fix this. I wanted my family. I felt blessed with my pregnancy because I had thought before that God would never allow me to have another child after the abortion. But I was more devastated at the thought of bringing another child into the turbulent mess our home had become.

Michael and I walked into the counselor's office feeling like this was our last chance to heal our relationship and move forward into a blissful marriage. She listened as I struggled to share my painful past, the abortion, our now-bitter relationship. After we finished, she looked at us and said, "Don't waste your time. There's no hope for you two."

She continued: "Until you individually repair your relationship with God and allow Him to heal you, you won't have a successful marriage. It's impossible to love another person when you desperately hate yourself."

At the therapist's suggestion, I went to a crisis pregnancy center for counseling and completed a post-abortion Bible study.

It took years for me to deal with my pain and regret.

I kept postponing the wedding. I just wasn't ready. I couldn't stop thinking about the abortion. It was a constant heartache.

Michael had become emotionally abusive and detached. I had sunk into a deep depression. I would just sit around the house.

Finally one night, as Michael sat, again pretending as though I was not there, I let it all out. "I was thinking about how it felt in the beginning. How we made our own home. How it felt to go through the day, thinking you were madly in love with me. I remember joy and contentment. I remember feeling like nothing and no one in the world could hurt me again. I remember the affairs you've had too, but each time I decided to focus on how lucky I was to have you as my provider. I remember sharing my life story with you about being abused by my son's father. I remember how angry that made you. 'How could someone be that cruel?' you asked while cupping my face in your hands. But I also remember you, more recently, looking into my eyes and saying nothing. I remember asking myself, why was I letting you hurt me too?"

I sat there rambling these sentiments from the depths of my soul and Michael simply looked on.

Months went by with little or no change. Michael was still distant; hanging out with friends every chance he got, leaving me and my son alone. The house was beautifully laid out, but it was empty. Empty of any kind of love that should warm the hearts of those who lived there. I contemplated leaving several times but couldn't. I needed the security and wanted a normal life for my children. I convinced myself that I had a good life and all was good. I knew there was someone else occupying his late nights, but I refused to give up my home and all I had invested in it.

Chapter 10
CLOUDS ON THE HORIZON

She's here!

After every storm comes a rainbow—a sentiment that couldn't be truer at that season in my life. We had gone for my thirty-six-week checkup. I was drained and tired. I was ready to get this over with. I was excited about having a daughter, but the thought that I was having this baby against the will of her father weighed heavy on my heart. He smiled from time to time and vaguely spoke of her, but I knew it was just to comfort me. I had lost hope, but for the sake of my children, I had to push through.

The day I went into labor, I had a major burst of energy. I had heard about this from so many women (including my own mom) during my first pregnancy, and, sure enough, I got it too. Despite my bump that got in the way of just about everything, in my own mind there wasn't anything I couldn't do. I was on fire!

I'm going to describe the day in quite a bit of (mundane) detail. Sunday, December 27, 1992, I was feeling antsy and distracted despite a large to-do list on my desk. After breakfast, I went on a long walk with my son to try to release the restless energy. I was having some pelvic pressure throughout the walk, but thought nothing of it since it had been happening on and off for a few weeks. By that evening, though, I knew that this time was different.

I started to time the contractions around midnight. The contractions were coming every 2–2.5 minutes already, lasting for 45–60 seconds, and felt very intense. I couldn't believe how quickly things progressed. I was scared. I'd had a cesarean with my son and had begged to do the same with my daughter, but the doctor wasn't having it.

"There's nothing preventing you from having a natural birth," she had said.

The contractions hurt. I had to breathe deeply to get through each one. I bounced on our exercise ball for a bit and then took a shower. Michael was a nervous wreck. He started packing last minute things like my nightgown, slippers, and journal. He knew not to forget the journal. That was my lifeline, the connection to my life journey. I had lots of them, as writing was therapeutic for me. It was now 1:30 a.m. I grabbed the journal that Michael had just placed in my overnight bag and I wrote, "I am humbled by labor already. Scared. I'm thinking an epidural sounds good right about now. I'm impressed though by how nice it feels when a contraction ends! Maybe I can get through this??" That was the last note I wrote to myself. After that I had my game face on—things got real, quickly.

Once we were certain I was in labor, we called the doctor. She instructed us to head to the hospital and said that she would meet us there. I started to freak out a bit. I was in so much pain. I recall yelling at Michael, "I want to get an epidural as soon as I get to the hospital."

Michael helped me into the car. Josiah was groggy from being awakened from his sleep. "Mommy's sorry," I said. "You can sleep in the car."

I had about three intense contractions during the car ride to the hospital. Michael seemed to hit *every* pothole in the road and each made the contractions more painful. I focused on my breathing techniques and handled them.

I called my best friend, Valerie. She had taken Lamaze classes with me when Michael couldn't be there, which was often. She answered, almost singing her question, "Are we ready?"

"Yes, can you come now?" I replied.

"I'm on my way," she said. I knew I needed more than Michael's support. Truth be told, I preferred for him to not even be there. As we approached the emergency room entrance, it was as if he'd read my thoughts.

"Let's get you checked in and I'll take Josiah to Aunt Clara's and come back."

I nodded. The nurse took me back to the examination room. Dr. Walker came shortly thereafter and checked my cervix. "Oh my." She seemed surprised. "You're just about ready. Do you want the epidural, or would you like to have her naturally?"

"Epidural! Please!" I am sure the people down the hall heard me beg.

Valerie made it just before I unraveled. She saw the look of despair on my face and began to coach me through the breathing techniques we had learned in class. It felt good having my friend there; she calmed my nerves. There's much to be said for having your bestie, a woman, there with you, especially when she had already been through it herself.

By six in the morning, the sun was preparing to rise and the contractions picked up to 1.5–2 minutes apart, lasting about 60–75 seconds. They also got a lot more intense on the pain scale. I started to cry during one of the contractions because I was so scared of what would happen next—and, subconsciously, about the labor itself.

Time went by slowly though. At 6 cm dilated, I started to feel desperate for relief. I asked when the doctor would give me the epidural. The pain was unbearable—epidural, laughing gas, extra-strength Tylenol, whatever. I wanted *all the drugs*. I was feeling major self-doubt at that point.

They put me on another bed and hooked me up to a monitor for twenty (long) minutes to check the baby's heart rate and monitor my contraction patterns. I disliked being confined to the bed and not being able to move around like I could at home. Finally, the nurse checked my cervix and found that I had progressed to 7 cm. I was absolutely *thrilled*. I would've danced on the bed if I wasn't in so much pain. All that laboring at home paid off. I felt like we might not be far off from meeting our baby girl.

But oh, there was plenty more to endure. Michael again wanted to leave and take our son to my aunt Clara's, thinking he would have time to make it back for the delivery. I was so over his reluctance to be there that I agreed that he should go. I couldn't bear the sight of him in the room, knowing that he didn't want any part of our daughter.

Moments after Michael exited the room, they whisked me down to labor and delivery. I was nervous about being a mom again, especially to a daughter, but the pain from the contractions was so intense I barely even noticed where I was. I was only concerned about getting through the pain.

Finally, some relief. The anesthesiologist arrived. He asked me my name and went over the procedure. I don't think I heard anything he said other than, "I need you to be very still. You will feel pressure and hear what sounds like a little thump and that's it." Before I could respond, it happened just as he said. Minutes later, I was on cloud nine. The nurse showed me the monitor and how to detect the contractions.

After an hour of laboring in the delivery room, I was checked and found to be completely dilated and ready to push. The nurse had her hand on my lower back and Valerie held my hand. She was praying the entire time. It would go rather quickly, I thought. I pushed and pushed but nothing happened. Take a deep breath; I did just that.

"PUSH!" Dr. Walker encouraged. "I can see her head." I felt a burning sensation and stopped dead in the middle of that push.

I screamed, "The medication is wearing off. I can feel it. What the heck? Did he not give me the full dose?" Now I was crying and afraid to push. Dr. Walker and the nurses were urging me to push; my friend was begging me to push.

"Come on Cilla, you got this. She's not going to just drop. You must push. She's ready to come out." Before I could argue with any of them, she was headed out on her own. I couldn't stop her and I was forced to complete the process. I pushed as hard as I could against my will. Then I heard a tiny voice that warmed my heart. She was here. I was tired—dead tired.

My baby girl, Alexus Tamara, made a grand entrance into the world, and for that I was grateful. Michael arrived hours later with a lame story that he was caught up talking with my aunt Clara. He said he didn't think I was going to have her that quickly. But I was done with his excuses. The warning signs were there quite early on. It's surprising how clear things seem in retrospect. But at the time, I was in love and I thought I could help him. I did help him for a while.

What I did was this: I changed my behavior to accommodate his. When I saw a problem about to happen, I pulled back and shut my mouth. I swallowed it (whatever *it* was at the moment), where a lot of women wouldn't (and shouldn't). So, in a way, we were the perfect partners. My behavior helped keep his behavior acceptable. Had I not bitten my tongue so many times, we would have exploded into many full-blown shouting matches. Nasty and volatile emotional abuse and perhaps, eventually, physical abuse. But I held back. Simply because I wanted it to work.

There were at least five or six instances in the ten or so years we were together where I didn't bite my tongue. Each time, I found myself on the receiving end of a toxic tirade that

I never forgot; abusive, bullying ranting is the best way to describe it.

This was the echo of the domestic violence that had gone on before in my previous relationship with David, except in my relationship with Michael, there was no physical abuse, no name-calling, no bad language. He knew where to draw the line and he thought that if he never crossed that fine line, all was well.

Michael's abuse would manifest in a much more insidious way: emotional manipulation; withdrawal of affection whenever I displeased him or whenever he couldn't get his way; mirroring, by accusing me of shouting at him when he was the one shouting at me; and financial abuse, his oft-repeated cry of "I pay the bills and the mortgage" to shut down any dissent from me, plus a control-freak attitude to joint finances that often had me secretly asking my parents for grocery money. Then there was the ever-present threat to go elsewhere for sex if I did not personally fulfill his quota. And he meant every word. My confidence was slowly leeched away.

I became like a dog keeping its head low to avoid confrontation. He claimed often that he loved me, but he did not behave as though he loved me. As a result, I did not trust him with my feelings and I did not feel loved. I coped by withdrawing into myself so that he couldn't get to me. This made him even more difficult to live with. He saw it as a withdrawal of my love. He retaliated by pointedly withdrawing his "love" from me. He made my life unpleasant. There were cold, stony silences that went on for weeks; nasty barbs directed at me in front of the children; and constant insinuations that I might be having an affair.

It's uncomfortable to live with someone who seems determined to punish you at every turn. And it's difficult to keep your bearings when you are constantly told that you are the one causing the problem.

I thought having our daughter would help. I thought she would soften his heart and change his mind. But eight years in, nothing had changed. I had gone through multiple affairs of his; each time, Michael convinced me that it never happened. Despite all the evidence—women calling our home, his late nights with the guys, hotel charges on the credit card statements—I chose to stay.

I kept trying to convince myself—even though the writing was on the wall—that things would work out. But then I would notice little inconsistencies about Michael's behavior. For instance, he became secretive about where he was going and who he was talking to all the time. I would always dismiss the thought of him being unfaithful to numb the pain. I convinced myself that I was the apple of his eye. The woman he came home to each night. The one who had his back. I was his go-to girl. I supported him in every area of his life.

Chapter 11
THAT CHRISTMAS

The phone rang. It was late in the afternoon, the day before Christmas. "I'm still at the mall, do you need anything?" Michael asked. I replied in the negative. I remember that that year I had a long Christmas list for him, most of which I knew he had already gotten. The one thing I longed for, though, was a new Seiko watch. I'd seen it while we were shopping at the mall for the kids. He'd played it off at the time. But surely, I figured, he's at the mall on Christmas Eve to get my watch.

Christmas was always a big deal for my family. We always exchanged gifts, but the greatest gift ever was my mom. She would gather the kids around the fireplace with her Santa hat on and read the story of Christ's birth. Then we would sing "Silent Night" and dance to the Jackson 5's song "Santa Claus Is Comin' to Town." So, not having Michael home bothered me.

I heard the garage open and my eyes lit up. I just knew he was going to try and surprise me. As he approached the staircase, I could see that his hands were empty. He came into the kitchen and planted a soft, gentle kiss on my lips. My heart nearly leapt out of my body. I had never felt this way and had never been so happy. He's trying to surprise me, I said to myself again.

We settled in for the night and watched movies into the wee hours of the morning. I finally fell asleep around four in the morning. I wouldn't get much sleep. I got up just a few hours later. The house was quiet. Michael was sound asleep. I was feeling uneasy about the night before and why it had taken him so long to get home after the mall had closed. I made my way to the living room where the lights were blinking on the seven-foot white Christmas tree. The floor was covered with gifts for the kids. I looked closer to see if I could find anything that resembled the size of a watch box. Nothing.

I don't know why I suspected foul play, but I grabbed the car keys off the wall and went downstairs to the garage. I peeked through the windows of Michael's car and voila—there it was—a nicely wrapped, gold package that looked like it could be a watch, with a neatly tied red bow, on the back seat. I smiled as I opened the car door. I knew he would get it, I said to myself as I backed out and softly closed the door again. He just didn't want me to see it under the tree.

Nothing mattered anymore. All my suspicions were gone. The spirit of Christmas was all over me. I pranced up the stairs, humming one of my favorites by Donny Hathaway:

Hang all the mistletoe,
I'm gonna get to know you better

This Christmas,
And as we trim the tree,
How much fun it's gonna be together,
This Christmas . . .

I pulled out the Santa Claus cookie cutter for the kids' pancakes. The aroma of crisp bacon filled the air. Tamara would be the first one up.

"Mommy, did Santa Claus come?"

"I don't know, love. Have you looked under the tree?"

She ran into the living room. Her eyes lit up as she screamed, "Santa was here, Mommy!" I just knew this was going to be the best Christmas ever for them. We had gotten everything on their list and more. All the commotion woke Josiah up and Michael was soon to follow.

There was so much excitement in the room with the kids that I almost forgot about my gift in the car. We let the kids open their gifts first. All the gifts had names on them, so once the kids were done ripping their gifts open, I gave Michael his gifts. He wasn't picky, so I usually dressed him in the latest style. That Christmas wouldn't be any different. As he unwrapped the cashmere wool sweater from Nordstrom with the matching cashmere scarf, I fixated on a small box under the tree wrapped in *101 Dalmatians* wrapping paper. The same paper I used to wrap some of our daughter's gifts.

I didn't recognize the gift. I turned my attention back to Michael, who was now trying to help Josiah open the packaging of his WWF wrestling figures: Sting and Macho Man Randy Savage. He was fascinated with wrestling.

Tamara had finished ripping her last gift open when she spotted the Dalmatian-wrapped gift under the tree. She ran and grabbed it, but just as she was about to rip it open, Michael yelled, "That's not yours li'l girl, that's Mommy's."

What? I looked at him awkwardly, and he smiled and said, "Open it."

This must be a joke, go get my gift out of the car, I said to myself. Then I thought, okay, this must be something from the kids. So, I smiled and opened my gift. My eyes must have been playing tricks on me. There, wrapped in some children's Dalmatian Christmas paper, was the Gold Seiko watch with diamonds around the face that I had been asking for!

"What the heck? Is this all I got?" I asked Michael.

"That's all you said you wanted, right?"

"Yes," I replied, but then screamed, "Wrapped in dog paper? Whose gift is that downstairs in the back seat of the car?" His eyes got big. You could have bought him for a dollar.

"That's Trey's gift for his girl," he prevaricated.

"You're lying!" I screamed. "Why is it in your car?"

"He accidently left it after we left the mall."

I knew he was lying, and, as much I wanted to slap the truth out of his mouth, I knew I couldn't. The kids were watching.

The voices in my head started to taunt me; cruel, hateful words began to form. How could I be so stupid, so naïve? All of the nights, working late and picking up extra shifts that didn't add up with the direct deposit posted in our joint bank account. How could I be so incredibly blind? The nights when he was so cold and distant. How could I not feel her in the bedroom with us? Who is *her*, you ask? Why, the other woman, of course.

We've all seen it, whether in someone else or in ourselves: A woman falls in love and, somewhere along the way, forgets herself and fades into half a person. Some way, somehow, the wants and needs of another human being become more important than her own. She disappears into herself—or, more accurately, into her new romance—not to return until the initial sense of magic fades. Falling head-over-heels in love is an exhilarating and exciting feeling, one that's all too easy to get caught up in whenever we're lucky enough to recognize the sensation. But while love and partnership can be amazing if you want to have those things, they should never come at the cost of your own sense of self.

That Christmas day, December 25, 1999, I accepted the truth. My heart fell down, fell out. **I felt it.** I heard it fall to the floor and shatter; or maybe that was the sound of the glass Cinderella Happily-Ever-After castle I had lived in for almost ten years, shattering. As it came crashing to the ground, it felt like millions of tiny shards of glass pierced my body. My chest felt as if an elephant was sitting on it, my breaths were coming in short gasps, my stomach churned, and I feared I would vomit.

All this as I stood in the living room staring at my babies, the only thing that mattered to me at that moment. I dismissed the pitiful-looking man with haunted, sorrowful eyes. The kids were now standing between us, waiting to wash their hands and eat the Christmas-themed breakfast with Santa Claus pancakes.

Desperately trying to keep the smile pasted on my face, I cheerfully said, almost singing, "Let's wash those hands and have some breakfast!" Anything to protect them from what I knew was coming.

Chapter 12
THE BREAKING POINT

All I could hear were whispers and the sirens blaring loudly outside of my home. I had barricaded myself in my bedroom. Peggy, the mom of my son's best friend, was pleading from the other side for me to open the door. There was a part of me that desperately wanted to, but the voice inside my head warned me otherwise.

Boom! The door collapsed and the officer shouted a command: "Put the knife down."

I froze. As I sat in the corner of my bedroom in a fetal position, my son begging and pleading with me to give the officer the knife that I clenched tightly in my hand, my heart ached and I didn't know why. A twelve-year-old girl, crying out for her mommy, but she wasn't there. "Mommy, Mommy," I sobbed uncontrollably.

The officer repeated the command. "Miss. Please put the knife down." The terror in my son's eyes broke my heart. He looked at me as if he didn't recognize me. His eyes pierced my soul as I lowered my hands. The officer, slowly and with caution, removed the weapon from my hands and placed his handcuffs on my wrists.

How does an eleven-year-old process the idea that his mom had experienced enough and contemplated ending her life? What would he think of me? The look in his eyes, as the paramedics tended to my superficial wound before placing me on the gurney, was crushing. The flashing lights, the noise of the fire truck's sirens, drowned out the noise in my head. I laid in the back of the ambulance gazing into the bright lights, wondering how I had arrived at this place in my life. After suffering years of betrayal, infidelity, emotional abandonment and mental abuse—I broke. I broke in a way that would nearly cost me my mind. I had given Michael all that I had, but it still wasn't enough and it would never be enough. I had loved another human being more than I loved myself. I thought that was the way it was supposed to be when you're in love.

Experiencing the hurt was inevitable. The depth of my love for Michael brought with it in equal measure the potential for pain and anguish. The pain associated with the love I thought I had was substantial and went beyond temporary feelings of grief and despair. The psychological distress had left me shattered.

I could clearly hear my mother's voice: "At some time or another in your life, you will come to a crossroads. A life-changing event that will change your life forever." This would be my crossroads.

I awakened in a room of bright lights, struggling to free my hands from the clinking noise they made with my every attempt to move. It seemed so surreal, almost like an out-of-body experience. I was confused and unaware of why I was lying there in a hospital bed in restraints. Both my hands and feet were fighting against the cold, stainless-steel cuffs, barely able to move. Once I realized that I was truly bound to the bed, I stopped struggling.

Then I noticed her. She had a notepad and was peering at me over the rims of her bifocals. She introduced herself as Dr. Williams. "Good morning," she said with a smile.

"Good morning," I whispered.

"How are we feeling?"

Was this intended to be a rhetorical question? "I'm okay," I replied.

"Good," said Dr. Williams. "Do you know where you are and why you're here?"

"No, ma'am."

She stood up and asked again, "Are you okay?" This made me wonder if I had answered incorrectly the first time.

I whispered, "I don't know."

She looked at me long and hard, as if to say, I believe you. "Well, you're at Swedish Medical Center in the psychiatric observation ward. You were brought in last night. Can you tell me what happened last evening?"

I looked at her with a blank stare; I couldn't remember. "No, ma'am," I responded.

Dr. Williams jotted a few notes on her pad. "The nurse has informed me that you have a relative by the name of Linda in the waiting room who wanted to let you know your mom is on her way."

"My mom? Why is Mom traveling all the way from Shreveport, Louisiana, to Seattle, Washington? What's going on?" I asked, afraid to hear the answer.

My body began to tighten and I felt totally out of control. It was as if my body was no longer mine. As the tears began to well in my eyes, I silently prayed: Lord, I know You are real and I know You answer prayers. Reveal Yourself to me right now. I am afraid and unsure of what is going on in my life right now. Lord, give me strength. Lord, help me.

I laid there in silence. The room was silent for several minutes and then Dr. Williams spoke. She gave me a watered-down version of what had happened the night before. "Priscilla, it appears that you had a nervous breakdown. In medical terms, a dissociative psychotic episode."

She explained this type of breakdown is a common defense and/or reaction to stressful or traumatic situations, severe childhood traumas, or the repeated trauma of abuse. She continued, "A dissociative disorder impairs the normal state of awareness and limits or alters one's sense of identity, memory, or consciousness."

Because she was not sure about the extent of my episodes, Dr. Williams was careful not to trigger a traumatic memory that could cause me more harm than good. She didn't divulge any more information. I laid there motionless, trying to absorb every word. Tears flowing, I softly asked Dr. Williams if she could have the cuffs removed.

She responded by asking a series of questions. "Are you having or have you ever had thoughts of suicide? Are you a threat to yourself or anyone else? Have you had thoughts of hurting yourself or anyone else?"

Where was she going with this line of questioning? Tears rolled down my face as I shook my head *no* to all the questions asked. I began to cry uncontrollably. I had no idea what was going on. Dr. Williams placed her hand on mine. She whispered softly, "If you will calm down, I'll have the officer outside the door remove the handcuffs." Officer? Was I under arrest for a crime that I had no memory of committing? Oh Lord, have mercy. Why was there an officer outside? What was going on? Breathe, Priscilla, I kept saying to myself.

A few moments later, a nurse came in to check my vitals. Dr. Williams explained that she had ordered a sedative to calm me down. "It's just a little something for the anxiety," she explained. I could feel my body going into a state of relaxation. I felt completely helpless and out of control of my normal faculties. After the nurse left the room, the officer came in and removed the cuffs that I'd been restrained with for the last twenty-four hours or more.

I tearfully explained to the doctor that I wasn't crazy and I honestly didn't understand what was going on. She repeated the story told to her and explained again that I had suffered a nervous breakdown. My eleven-year-old son had found me in a state that frightened him and he called his best friend's mom, Peggy, who called 911.

I tried to recall the moments that lead up to this to no avail. Struggling to remember what had transpired just twenty-four hours ago, all I drew was a blank. I did remember arguing with my daughter's father and asking him to leave my home. It had been a tumultuous year of finally deciding to leave Michael and beginning the process of extricating myself from him, and I had had enough, overwhelmed by going back and forth to court to settle the sale of the home and establish child support. It had taken years, but I was ready to break free from the jail cell of all the emotional and mental abuse I had willingly endured for more than a decade of my life.

It didn't start out this way, I kept telling myself. He was my prince charming. He had rescued me from the pits of hell. From the hands of David. Surely he would never do anything to hurt me, is what I told myself throughout those eleven years.

My mind raced back through all the years I had suffered in silence, in a relationship with a man who wasn't capable of loving. He didn't have the inner capacity to care about anyone but himself. My life was penetrated and broken down strategically over the years and I became engrossed in him. I had become a willing participant in the methodical breaking of my own mind, so subtle that I couldn't see it happening. At that very moment, I realized a dark force was working through him to get to me. Ephesians 6:12 had manifested and I had been fighting something far bigger than me: "For we wrestle not against flesh and blood, but against principalities, against powers, against the rulers of the darkness of this world, against spiritual wickedness in high places." Then my inner voice began to speak to me. The same voice that I often blew off. We all have that inner voice that tells us that something just isn't right. It is almost like a sixth sense trying to alert you of the dangers ahead should you continue down that road. That quiet voice that often whispered, *"Trust Me."*

How had I arrived at this point? The last few years of constant harassment and non-stop court appearances had taken their toll. I was drained, exhausted, tired, depressed, and on the verge of breaking down. I was diagnosed with depression and anxiety. I was losing weight at a rapid speed because I couldn't eat. I cried every day. Never really opened up to anyone. I had no confidence whatsoever. I'd lost so much weight. I couldn't cope anymore. I was anxious and tired, stressed and weary. It all added up until I had my breakdown.

God spoke yet again: *"Trust Me."* I had given Michael so much power over the years. I had endured years of physical and mental abuse with David, and the emotional manipulation and psychological abuse was not what I had envisioned for my life with Michael. I was ready for a change. Even though I had stayed in an abusive relationship for years, stayed with a man who treated me worse than anyone ever could, mentally, I was very proud of myself for finally leaving, no matter how long it took. Anyone going through this or having been through this knows that domestic violence wears you down; it kills your self-esteem and you literally feel you are trapped and that there's no way out.

After I left, I knew I could never go back, because if I did, I wouldn't be able to get out again. With the help of friends, I stayed away from his pleas and begging, his promises that this time would be different. It was hard, but nowhere near as hard as actually being with him. I got counseling and talked to the few friends I had left who were supportive, and by just letting it out and telling someone, I felt a weight had been lifted and I stopped minimizing the abuse.

But then things got worse again. I had become so full of hatred and resentment toward Michael that it had taken me to what seemed like the point of no return. I was so consumed with hating him and letting that hatred eat away at me, at my life and health, that I drowned out the voice of the Holy Spirit speaking to me. Looking back, I can see God had been nudging me the entire time and I chose to ignore Him. Yes, I had failed to listen to God. And in doing so, my life went out of control. I was as bad as Eve in the garden.

Chapter 13
STARTING TO HEAL

It seemed like I had been sitting in that room in the psychiatric ward for an eternity. I was on pins and needles, my mind racing as I awaited the results from the psychological evaluation. I began to cry out, "Lord, I am giving this pain to you. I don't know what to do. Letting go is so hard, but for my sake I must walk away. Lord, give me the strength to move!"

When I stood up, my legs felt like overcooked noodles. My feet were sealed to the concrete floor. I kept telling myself to move but I couldn't. My life had just shipwrecked and it was time to sort through the debris of all the mistakes I had made. I could not do it alone. Feelings of helplessness and hopelessness shrouded my spirit and I felt like all hope was lost. I had come to the end of my rope, at the bottom of a deep pit, and the voice of the enemy had me believing things would never get better.

But suddenly, in that hospital room, another inner voice began to speak to me:

Do not be anxious about anything, but in everything by prayer and supplication with thanksgiving let your requests be made known to God. And the peace of God, which surpasses all understanding, will guard your hearts and your minds in Christ Jesus. (Philippians 4:6–7)

Was this the voice I had been running from all those years? The voice that warns us that something just isn't right. The voice of the Holy Spirit that alerts you of the dangers ahead, should you continue down this path. Then God spoke again: *"So do not fear, for I am with you; do not be dismayed, for I am your God. I will strengthen you and help you; I will uphold you with my righteous right hand."* (Isaiah 41:10)

My spirit was in a tug-of-war with what God had just spoken; I was still buying into the idea that my life was worthless, even though it was in direct conflict with my core beliefs. I was facing a feud inside my own heart and mind. On the one hand, I was struggling with my sense of worthlessness. On the other hand, I was telling myself I believed in God and His son Jesus Christ. I know that because of Him I can have hope. "Father, God," I cried out. "I am standing on your promise!"

In Romans 8:28 it is said, "And we know that all things work together for good to those who love God, to those who are the called according to His purpose."

As I sat on the edge of the bed contemplating what to say to God next, my eyes fell upon a book in the corner of the room. Where had it come from? I hadn't noticed anything in the room aside from the chair and the single, framed bed with the crinkled white linen sheets, but there it was. I picked up the book and there it was, as bold as day, the Holy Bible. I clutched it tightly and held it close to my heart, clinging to it as if it were life support, the oxygen I needed to breathe new life into my current situation. At that moment, I truly felt and knew beyond a shadow of a doubt that the presence of God was in the room. The Holy Spirit spoke clearly and directed me to 2 Chronicles 7:14:

> If my people, who are called by my name, will humble themselves and pray and seek my face and turn from their wicked ways, then I will hear from heaven, and I will forgive their sin and will heal their land.

For my healing to take place, I had to come to a place of total surrender. When your soul has been violated only God can heal you. When you have given away pieces of your soul repeatedly and you feel like you have nothing left, when your soul is depleted of all the strength needed to live, it's time to let go and let God perform open-heart surgery. It is time to begin the healing process, time to reclaim your soul and allow God to be the driving force in mending the wounds of your soul so you can become whole again.

As I got up off my knees from praying, the door opened. Dr. Williams, the nurse, and the psychologist who had administered the psych evaluation walked in. Dr. Williams spoke first. She advised me that, by law, they could have me involuntarily committed for up to seventy-two hours for observation as a precautionary measure. However, after consulting with Dr. Rice, the head psychologist, they felt confident I was not a threat to myself or anyone else and I could be released into the care of my cousin Linda until my mother arrived.

Oh, the power of prayer! It is soul-satisfying to know that God is mindful of us and ready to respond when we place our trust in Him. There is no place for fear when we place our trust in the Almighty. Those who do not hesitate to humble themselves in seeking divine guidance through prayer will find comfort. Though persecutions come, in prayer we can find reassurance, for God will speak peace to the soul. That peace, that spirit of serenity, is life's greatest blessing.

My knees were trembling as the nurse read the discharge instructions. Within an hour, it was done. I was released and on my way home. I walked slowly through the hospital parking garage, silently praying and thanking God. I settled in my seat and put on my seatbelt in anticipation of the long drive, expecting a lecture from my cousin on the way. She had been with me through thick and thin over the last few years. I laid my head back, my mind drifting back to what had happened. As I sat there, however, my thoughts took a downward turn: You're crazy! You're not worthy! You tried to take your life! Your family thinks you are crazy. What are your children going to think about you? What will your friends think? Surely they will find out.

Tears filled my eyes as my heart raced and anxiety began to set in again. I was so overwhelmed by everything going on that I had forgotten my mom was coming. I started dwelling on a new cause of worry: How could she afford to fly out so soon? As far as I knew, my mom was not in a position, financially, to pay for a flight from Shreveport to Seattle on such short notice. But then I calmed myself. God provides, I thought, smiling.

The drive from the hospital to my home took about forty-five minutes. I pulled myself together enough to call and check on my babies. I was a bit nervous because I didn't know just how much they had witnessed the night before. The phone rang twice and then Peggy picked up. "Hi, Peggy," I said, embarrassed.

"Hi, Priscilla," Peggy replied. I could hear the smile in her voice. We made small talk before she put Josiah on the phone. The excitement in his voice reassured me that he was fine.

"Mom, are you at home?" he asked.

"In a few minutes, baby," I said.

The sound of his voice soothed my heart and warmed my spirit. I smiled and told him how much I loved him and that I would see him the next day. As soon as I hung up with Josiah,

I called my girlfriend Valerie, as she had taken Tamara home with her, but before she could answer I dropped the phone. We had pulled up in front of my home and there were several cars that I did not recognize parked in my driveway. On the side of one of the vehicles, in bold black and white letters, it read "Kent Police." My heart dropped. Why were the police at my home? How did they even know I was on my way home? I slowly opened the car door. As I stepped out of the car, I saw a full-figured woman wearing a tan blouse and brown pants. I immediately recognized my mom. I wondered, worried, how she had made it to Seattle that fast. My palms were sweating and I began shaking uncontrollably. I stopped in my tracks, unable to move.

My mother came to me, grabbed me, and held me in her arms. I broke down again. She stroked my back and told me it was going to be all right. I asked her why the police were at the house. She explained that there had been an incident—attempted arson—at the house that Michael and I owned, and that Michael had given my name to the police as a person of interest. Of all the things that had just transpired in the last forty-eight hours, this was the most frightening to me. Could my nervous breakdown be taken as a sign of guilt over such a horrendous crime? I am not that crazy, I kept telling myself, struggling to listen to the detective as she laid out the accusations. My mom stepped in and explained to the detective that I had just been released from the hospital and was not up to being questioned just yet. She insisted that they wait a few days and give me time to obtain legal counsel. The detective seemed agitated and tried to convince my mother that they were only there to exclude me from the list of suspects by administering a lie detector test. Suspects?

Now, I cannot fully comprehend the physical or spiritual suffering that Jesus endured, but in that moment in particular I could certainly relate to the passing of the cup: "Going a little farther, he fell with his face to the ground and prayed, 'My Father, if it is possible, may this cup be taken from me. Yet not as I will, but as you will.'" (Matthew 26:39)

I stood there in disbelief. Never in a million years would I have expected this from Michael. I knew he was angry about me leaving, but never would I have thought it would come to this. I was humiliated and hurt, to say the least. How could he subject me to such egregious accusations? This seemed at first too much for me to bear, but my asking God's will to be done in my life then became a true testament of my faith. I had decided to trust God in all of what was happening, and if He allowed it, then there had to be a reason. I repeatedly told myself that I had to trust God's purpose and His plan, even though I couldn't fully understand it. I had to follow God's lead. Complete submission was required.

I looked at my mom. I could see the anguish in her eyes. I felt sorry for her. Sorry that my burden had become hers. I was causing her so much pain. I looked at the detective and then at my mom again. "Mom," I said, "I don't need a lawyer. I haven't committed any crime, and if it will make all of this go away today, I'll go take the test."

I asked the detective to provide me the information on where I needed to go. My cousin Linda stood there quietly, and when I looked at her, I could tell she already knew what I was thinking. Clothed in the hospital gown, sweats, and a pea coat, I crawled into the back seat of my cousin's car. Mom would take the front. There was nothing but silence for the first few minutes of the drive. Then Mom pulled out one of her gospel CDs. James Cleveland came on and mom turned up the volume. Mom sang along, and it seemed so surreal as James Cleveland sang out: "I don't feel no ways tired, I've come too far from where I started from. Nobody told me that the road would be easy, I don't believe He brought me this far to leave me."

The tears ran down my face; that was sure confirmation for me. God didn't bring me this far to leave me. We made it to the station in less than an hour. As we entered the building I felt a cold rush of air. The fire detective was already there and asked my mom and my cousin to wait in a closed room. She then led me down the hallway to a small room where an officer was sitting in the corner. The officer glanced at my attire and then looked up at me as if to say, "Really, lady?"

The officer advised me that the test being administered was of my own free will. He informed me of the specific issues being investigated and advised me of my constitutional rights.

I was given an opportunity to ask questions or share any concerns before the test began. I had none. I just wanted to get it over with and get out of that place.

I was running on less than five hours of sleep in a forty-eight-hour period. I was nervous and unable to shake the unreality of being in that tiny little room, getting ready to undergo a lie detector test, all because my ex wanted to get back at me for reasons that to this day are unknown. He was the one, after all, who had cheated and lied, which caused the demise of the relationship.

Once the preliminary procedures were complete, a blood pressure cuff was placed on my arm and a small rubber tubing across my chest and abdomen to monitor my respiratory activity. Electrodes were placed on my fingers to monitor sweat gland activity. The officer explained what each thing did as he attached the probes.

I remember praying silently: Lord, thank you for dying on the cross, because the cross before me at this moment is too much for me to bear. As I ended my prayer, the examination officer looked at me with sad eyes. He apologized. I guess the fire detective notified him of my recent release from the hospital, but that I had still agreed to come and take the test to be excluded as a suspect.

Tears filled my eyes yet again. I could tell he wished he didn't have to do it, but he did. It was his job. It was time to start the test, and I felt like I had cried a river.

It wasn't as bad as I thought it would be and it didn't take too long. When it was over, the examiner looked at me with empathy and said, "You passed." He apologized profusely for the inconvenience and wished me well.

"God, great God," I said as I opened the door to leave. The fire investigator met me midway down the hall. She gave me the same look of empathy the examiner had given me and she too apologized and thanked me for coming down to the station. As I approached the front entrance of the building, I saw my mom. She was pacing back and forth, praying and praising! Oh, the power of a praying mother! I was no longer a person of interest in the arson case. I was, however, still deeply hurt, and I didn't understand why Michael would accuse me of such a horrendous crime. It was gut-wrenching, but that chapter of my life, the abuse and all that came with it, was now over.

I would learn years later that David was released from prison after serving only three and a half years of his five-year sentence. His relationship with my son Josiah is nonexistent to this day. Michael married his mistress and they have two children together. His relationship with the kids remains strained. Josiah cut off all communication with him years ago and my daughter is struggling to maintain her relationship with him.

Chapter 14
AFTER IT'S OVER, IT'S NOT OVER

It was 2001 and my kids and I had comfortably transitioned to Dallas, Texas. It was hard for me to accept the fact that I had gone from one toxic situation to another in my previous relationships. I was disappointed and angry with myself for my poor choices in men. It didn't make sense that a beautiful and smart young lady would allow herself to go through that type of hell—twice. I questioned every intention of the guys I'd meet before I finally decided to just work on me. I decided to find out who Priscilla was and what would make me happy. I turned my focus to myself and my kids.

Starting over was going to be a journey, but one I was willing to take with the help of the good Lord. While working on this new leg of my journey, I spent a lot of time flying back and forth from Dallas to Seattle, in court with Michael. It wasn't enough that he had nearly wreaked havoc in our lives and purposely tried to drive me insane, he was also determined to ruin me financially.

Practically every other month or so, I was summoned to appear in King County Superior Court for child support and visitation matters. Michael really wasn't interested in visitation, but that's what he needed to do—I believe—to still maintain some degree of control. Instead of letting the daunting processes wear me down, though, I used the experience to help me understand myself and to pour effort into helping my children. They needed me. We had settled in our new apartment and they were adapting well to their new environment, but they still had questions about what had happened. I never spoke ill of their father, but I would answer them honestly when they would ask, "Why did Daddy leave?"

"Sometimes Moms and Dads can't see eye to eye. Sometimes it is best for Mommy and Daddy to live separately, in order to get along and be nice to each other," I explained.

Tamara didn't really understand. She would go on and on asking why. "But why, Mommy?" she would ask. "Don't you like Daddy?"

Josiah, on the other hand, was always quiet. He didn't show any emotion one way or the other. Even when I'd ask him how he felt, he would shrug his shoulder and say, "I'm okay." I can only imagine the hurt and frustration Michael's betrayal caused him.

It was a long and painful journey. I was still having anxiety about the transition.

I felt alone most of the time. Even with the kids and their daily bickering, I was lonely. But the loneliness was nothing compared to the absolutely agonizing emptiness I experienced with Michael. My home became my sanctuary, my place of peace and tranquillity. I didn't have that when I was with Michael or David.

I spent a lot of my time studying the word of God. My best friend Lorna was my rock. She showed me what real friendship looked like. She poured into me spiritually. She was my accountability partner. I had begun to embrace me through daily affirmations and by understanding who I was in Christ. I would memorize Bible verses that resonated with what was going on in my present in hopes of finding my way to a more peaceful life.

I enjoyed being single and found that I was far too traumatized, still, to get out and date. I had trust issues. I didn't trust myself and thought I would end up picking guys who were like my exes. Time was so important for my healing. It was a painful jump off that cliff, but I did it and I made it. Now I had to spread my wings and fly. It was time for me to soar.

"You are strong and you will make it," I kept telling myself. I wrestled with the residue of the brokenness that remained. I wrestled with the guilt of being a single parent, that my children were not being raised in a two-parent home. Yes, all my brokenness was real, and it would remain. But that did not change the fact that God was still God. I had to be still and know that He was God. I had to surrender and stand firm in the promises of God—that, even though I was broken, I could still find His peace. The peace that surpasses all understanding, even through brokenness, remained.

As I continued on my journey to start over, I also looked back on the first time I was broken, when my cousin sexually assaulted me back when I was twelve. It took me years to begin to come to terms with it, before I started to seek God in prayer and hold fast to His love for me. I had been totally dependent on God to get me through my teen years. Even at such an early age, God was trying to show me how to heal when my life was shattered. While I came to realize that God sometimes allows undesirable things to happen to good people, I had trouble applying that to myself.

For years as an adult, I continued to hold on to the belief that the abuse at the hands of my cousin was my fault. I felt an increasing need to rationalize why it was my fault. And it wasn't enough to just say it was my fault because I was a horrible person or that I did something, or even that I deserved it. I needed concrete facts to back up exactly why I believed it was my fault, which may sound strange to some. Why would I want to find concrete reasons to prove that the abuse was my fault? Yet despite the perceived illogicality of this, I looked for reason after reason to prove that it had all happened because of me. I feared sharing with anyone the traumatic events that took place back in 1978. I feared the blame and judgement that I worried would come along with the knowledge of the molestation and rape. I still heard and believed his words: "No one will believe you."

Back when I was first struggling to come to terms with what happened, I felt like God was silent in hearing my prayers when I so desperately needed to hear from Him. I needed someone, anyone, my mom, a friend, just someone to say, "Priscilla, you don't deserve what happened to you. God doesn't approve of any man who abuses others."

My desperation would fall on deaf ears because I hadn't told anyone and, apparently, God wasn't listening either. I was ready to move on with my life, and yet I was still struggling as I entered into adulthood. I had convinced myself that, as an adult, I could face what had happened. I was convinced I could protect myself and never allow anyone else to violate me in that way again.

One long night, when I was facing a dark night of the soul, I began to pray and ask God to comfort me and heal the wounds of my heart and my mind from the inside out. And as I began to cry out, the Holy Spirit began to minister to my spirit. God spoke to my spirit so clearly. *"I love you. You are not a victim! You are in fact victorious through Jesus Christ. I beseech you to find it in your heart to forgive those who hurt you. Just as I have forgiven you, my daughter."*

My eyes filled with tears. "Lord, why?" I cried. "How can I forgive and forget all of the pain?" I sat in that dark, quiet room. Then God spoke: *"Forgiving people who have hurt you doesn't mean you forget how they hurt you or that you give them the opportunity to hurt you again. Forgiving them means you make peace with what happened."* Forgiving means you acknowledge the wound, give yourself permission to feel the pain and understand why that pain can no longer serve you. It means you let go of the hurt and resentment so you can begin to heal and move on.

Dear reader, you may have suffered sexual abuse as a child as well. If this is you, please understand that I wrote this book with you in mind. As survivors of childhood sexual abuse, we often grow up blaming ourselves for the abuse. I know that I always blamed myself for what happened that summer.

I believed that the abuse happened because of something I did or didn't do. In my mind, that was as factual as the Earth being round. As a child, I was taught to respect older siblings and relatives. So when I was told to keep my mouth shut and that no one would believe me, I took it to heart and believed that, for whatever reason, it was my fault. When you think something long enough, you don't question the validity of it; it just is. That is how I felt for many years. I was to blame. End of story. However, that is not the end of the story, because I was not to blame! Your abuse was not your fault, no matter what your abuser told you. You can come up with as many reasons as you like as to why you're to blame, but not one of them will stand when exposed to closer scrutiny.

I believed that the reason I was hurt so badly was simply because it was what I deserved. I felt I deserved it because I was bad, worthless, pointless, nasty, ugly, stupid, and any other negative adjective you can think of. I'm sure many of you can identify with this. I felt that it was not what I did that made me bad; it was simply who I was. I honestly believed that nothing I did could make me better. I believed that I was inherently bad. I concluded that I was treated badly simply because of who and what I was. If you have felt this way, please know that these feelings are an effect of the abuse you experienced, not a statement of the truth. I understand your pain and the shame associated with being abused. I want you to know that you should not be ashamed, because you did *nothing* wrong. Regardless of what your abuser said to you, it was *not* your fault. No one deserves to be hurt in such a way.

Maybe you have family secrets. Maybe you are struggling to keep the faith and find it hard to be obedient to God's word. Trust me, as the Bible promises in 2 Timothy 2:13, God is and will always show Himself to be faithful. God may seem silent or absent today, but His purpose will become loud and clear in the future: for us to let go of having life our way and to live in Christ and trust in His way.

But God:

Genesis 50:20: You intended to harm me, but God intended it for good to accomplish what is now being done, the saving of many lives.

The art of surviving the painful moments of our past is through living in the now; the present moments of our lives. We need to learn how to respond to God with a "Yes, Lord" when the doors are open and a "Yes, Lord" when the doors are closed. We need to continually declare, as in Psalm 40, "Lord, I trust You and the decisions You have made for my life. Thank you for bringing me out of the miry clay and setting my feet upon a rock to stand."

This is the epitome of trusting God with our whole heart. When God allows painful betrayals to happen in our lives, He does so for a reason. I believe God will only allow what works for our good. Sometimes the betrayal ushers us into the next level of consecration, a level none of us could dare reach on our own.

As I continued to work through my past and reevaluate my life, I remembered the times I had tried to leave God out of the equation while on my quest for peace. My soul longed for it, but each time I tried to do it on my own, God would reel me back in. I specialized in looking for love in all the wrong places. And when I say all the wrong places, I mean anywhere God's rules were not necessarily a strong foundation for living. That is the relationship I would jump into, heart and spirit first. The wrong places became comfortable places for me because, truth be told, I was mad at God, and I wasted years of my life running away from Him. My aunt Agnes was right in her comment to me several years prior: I was running from the call that God had on my life. In this new place, this relationship with me and God, I continued to fast and pray. Humbling myself before God, I began to see life's trials as blessings and to weigh them from God's perspective and not mine.

That perspective is this: God allowed the trials in my life to help me grow up and to mature in Him. In other words, God was telling me, *"You will never grow in your walk with Me without trials. I use your trials to be your teacher and to make you into the person I called you to be."* I began to realize that if God hadn't allowed me to be broken, I would have never become the strong woman of faith He intended. I am who I am today because I experienced and persevered through the trials and testing. At the end of the day, God knew—and knows—exactly what He's doing in all our lives.

Now here's the lesson for you and me: We must trust God! The sovereign God knows what is necessary for us to experience in our lives and how much to permit to mature us. It really is amazing that, the moment we fall into a trial that is out of our own control, we begin to beg God to get us out of whatever we're in. Or, we demand to know what's wrong. When we are really anxious, we tell God we'll be fine if He'll just take it away. What we never stop to consider is what God might be doing—trying to change you and me, *not* the circumstances! He may (and He will) change the circumstances that trouble us, but in the meantime, He is trying to teach you (and me) lessons that will transform our lives. We'll miss the blessing by constantly begging Him to change the circumstances and not giving Him a chance to speak to us!

In hindsight, I realized that David was abusive from the start. At the time, though, I did not understand what was happening. I was nineteen years old and very innocent. So, during the first incident where he grabbed my arm, I wondered, sensed it was wrong, and yet dismissed it. I thought I was strong enough to stop the abuse. I thought I was strong enough to stop David and Michael. I didn't know how to drink, I didn't know how to take drugs, I didn't know how to smoke, but I did know how to force myself to keep moving along, silently killing myself on the inside. But once I left, it hit me like a ton of bricks—leaving was not the end of my story.

The abuse profoundly colored my life even after I managed to safely escape and begin to rebuild my life; there was the aftermath to walk through. At first, I couldn't sleep most nights. I had lost my faith and was convinced that the world was not a safe place. I was perpetually suspicious. Just like how a wild animal who has survived the terror of a forest fire recognizes the unpleasant smell of smoke faster than one who has not, a woman who has survived domestic violence sees warning signs and becomes determined to protect herself from further danger.

It had been five years since I left, and I still didn't have any idea how to reassemble the broken pieces of my life. Only then did I realize how deeply I had been betrayed. I learned about the depravity that characterized my abusers' behaviors. Thus, I had a strong urge to build a protective armor around my heart. I didn't think I could ever trust anyone ever again. I isolated myself in a hopeless place and I was very, very unhappy.

The realization that I was duped and manipulated generated strong feelings of shame, guilt, and confusion. I questioned my ability to discern good from evil. I beat myself up and sometimes I became my own worst enemy.

It was so important for me to acknowledge that all the emotions I was feeling were normal and that it was okay to experience them. I tried to rush through the recovery process after David and thus fell for Michael. It is impossible to rush through recovery. It is possible, however, to recover if you stay engaged with the process.

It was critical for me to be very gentle with myself and, more importantly, become my own best friend. I began to speak positive affirmations and make deliberate efforts to stop negative thoughts as soon as they tried to creep in. This was a very challenging path toward self-forgiveness and self-love, but it was necessary.

I had to internalize some truths. I trusted the wrong men because I did not know how to identify such monsters. The abuse was never *my* fault. When I began to listen to my heart more carefully, I discovered something deep within that is extremely valuable—my intuition.

Patiently facing the pain, forgiving and loving yourself, tuning in to your gut feelings, and developing appropriate confidence in yourself as a unique and capable individual: that is how you begin to trust again.

I found great joy in my life after I discovered my own worth and began trusting in it. While I couldn't guarantee that I'd never be hurt again, I was open to loving again. I believe we all have doubts and insecurities; all of us are imperfect beings and we all make mistakes. Although future pain is inevitable, future entanglements with abusive men are not. Yes, I might encounter them, but I can tell you with certainty, I will spot them quickly and not allow them into my space.

My sisters, when you realize how special you truly are, your life will become richer; you will make better decisions and you will establish loving, meaningful connections with others. And when you have faith in yourself, that is how you rebuild your faith in humanity. Trust me, there is hope and happiness to be found on the other side of the darkness. Just remember, it comes from *within*.

Chapter 15

FREEDOM: THE POWER OF FORGIVENESS

It was July of 2010 when my fiancé (now my husband) mentioned a women's conference that was coming soon at his church called "Desperate for Jesus!" The theme resonated with my spirit. I was *desperate* for anything that would take away my anger, bitterness, and inability to forgive the men who had hurt me. I had been harboring resentment for years. While I boldly confessed with my mouth that I had forgiven them, my heart held on to the fact that they didn't deserve my forgiveness. Desperate for Jesus is what I was, and it didn't take long for me to take him up on his offer. We logged on to the website and registered that day.

Although the conference was weeks away, I laid in bed, staring at the ceiling, wondering: what does that look like? What does it mean to be desperate for Jesus? Does it mean we only cry out in desperation when all hell is breaking loose in our lives? Do we relax and go into cruise control mode when things are going good in our lives? At that time in my life, I was feeling like the woman in the Bible with the issue of blood, the one who was healed by touching the hem of Jesus' robe, who demonstrated to us how to obtain the healing power of God: by the grace of Jesus Christ through faith that produces wholeness. I am convinced that God led my husband to bring me to "Desperate for Jesus" for the purpose of healing. I expected to hear from God in a mighty way in the weeks to come. I knew my deliverance was on the way!

As I turned off of Hampton Road onto Camp Wisdom, I grew weary. It was almost seven o'clock in the morning and there was bumper-to-bumper traffic. I hadn't seen anything like it since attending the Maze and Frankie Beverly concert at Nokia. The police were directing traffic, while women who had already found parking walked alongside the rows of cars. My weariness turned to excitement! I felt the spirit of God and I knew the conference was going to be life-changing for me. Once I found a parking spot, I hopped on the shuttle and made my way to the back, sitting in one of three seats remaining. I was filled with excitement and expectancy. As we neared the east side of the sanctuary, the lines were wrapped around the building. I remember thinking: who in the world is speaking at this conference? I had only been attending the church since meeting my now-husband, so I had no history and nothing to go on, other than my husband bragging about his church and the awesome man of God, Pastor Tony Evans.

I was in awe as I walked up to the check-in table. All the women were smiling and greeting me with so much love. It felt like a family reunion, and I was reconnecting with all of my long-lost family members. As I walked into the foyer, there were vendors of all sorts. T-shirts, fragrances, candles, books, and more. I slowly walked around and soaked up all the love and embraced all the hugs. There were over a thousand ladies in attendance.

As I entered the sanctuary, the praise and worship team was building up the ladies' fervor for the Lord. Yes, the presence of the Lord was in that place. There were prayer warriors praying at the altar. I quickly found a seat, one near the middle, but right where I could see the stage. Minutes later, the doors closed and the lights dimmed. It was show time, I thought to myself, and boy was I ready.

The introduction was powerful, and Priscilla Shirer, the host of the conference, had us pumped. The power of the Holy Spirit was in the room, and, as she prayed, I could sense God moving. I knew then that I was destined to be in this place, and I knew there was something greater to come!

We continued in praise and worship. I ushered my Father in as the presence of the Holy Spirit was having its way in the sanctuary.

As I closed my eyes and began to enter His presence, my eyes filled with uncontrollable tears. I slowly stretched my hands toward heaven and cried, "Lord, I need You, come into my heart, remove this pain, take the burdens of my past and help me to let go, help me to release my abusers. I don't want to feel like this, take the hatred away. Lord, I'm tired, I'm drained. Lord, I need You to help me." I didn't realize that I was so out of tune with what was going on around me until, when I opened my eyes, I saw that all the ladies were seated and I was the only one still standing. I could hear the music still playing as the speaker softly entreated the assembly to let the Lord have His way. Other women began to praise me, and then I was surrounded by women who began to lay their hands on me and cry out to God on my behalf.

It was powerful. It was overwhelming, yet humbling. I had never been in a women's conference with so many woman standing in agreement on another's behalf. My body began to tremble and I felt chills all over. Surely it was the Holy Spirit moving through me.

I could feel the shackles falling and the chains being broken. I visualized all the men that had abused me and violated my trust. I saw them all so clearly. Then, like a father speaking to his daughter in love, I heard the voice of God saying, *"Release them. Release them. They can no longer hurt you, my daughter. Daddy's here. I got you. It's okay to let it go. Release them. Forgive them, right now. Forgive yourself for carrying the burden of what they did to you. You did nothing wrong, this was not your fault. Let it go. You can stop carrying the guilt and shame for the men that abused you, that abused your trust. Let it go. You are free. No longer will you walk around with your head down because of the sins committed against you by others. You're a daughter of the King. Daddy's here."*

I began to praise God like I had never praised Him before. I danced like King David did in the Bible and shouted with a voice of triumph. I was free! Free from being molested at the age of twelve, free from being abused, free from being controlled, free from the lies and manipulation, free from deception. I was free!

As the praise and worship began to come to an end, I remember the host going over the program and giving instructions to the ladies about the individual sessions we had registered for. I sat still, basking in my deliverance. I didn't want that moment to end. I felt like if it came to an end, so would my deliverance. I didn't want a temporary fix; I needed permanent deliverance, to be free—once and for all.

I don't remember hearing the host dismiss the women for our breakout sessions, but as I made my way across the street, my heart still full and my mind tangled up in what I had just experienced, God spoke again and said *"release them and forgive them."* I knew I had let the incidents go, but God knew that, in my heart, I hadn't fully released my abusers. He knew that, deep down inside, that little twelve-year-old girl was still angry. He knew that the twenty-year-old mother was still scared of what could have been. He knew that the twenty-six-year-old mother of two was still broken from the mental abuse.

As I settled in my seat, I couldn't help but notice the room was packed. Wall to wall, women; some ready to share their stories; others, like myself, waiting for another breakthrough. I scanned the room to see the faces of the women; a lot of them looked like me: broken, alone, defeated, and longing to be delivered.

The speaker began the session by sharing her own story of abuse. You could hear a pin drop, the room was so silent. All eyes were on the tall, brown-skinned woman who graciously poured her heart out. Then, story after story, every woman in the room shared their stories of sexual abuse, physical abuse, emotional abuse, verbal abuse; you name it, and we had a sister in the room with a story about it.

Sister depression was there, sister abuse was there, sister low self-esteem was there, sister abortion was there. All the sisters were in the house that day!

I was absolutely stunned at the number of women who had walked a mile in my shoes; being sexually abused seemed to be a norm. Deeply moved by all the anguish these ladies had endured, I was equally impressed by their integrity and their ability to love and create love after all they had been through.

The beauty, the courage, and the strength it took for them to stand before a group of women and share their stories of brokenness filled my soul. This would be my deliverance; the healing process was moving in a liberating way. Here we were, woman of different races, diverse backgrounds, from all walks of life, and yet we were gathered in this safe place to face our individual pain and anger and heal our brokenness.

Just being in the presence of so many broken souls and having the opportunity to hear their stories and feel their pain was profoundly healing for me. I am sure the women who registered for that session, like myself, came with no intention to be as transparent and trusting as they were. We all simply wanted to become whole again. I wanted to be free to live again. I longed to cast off my emptiness, to become so full of myself that my overflow would be more than enough to fill up a few more women in my lifetime. It was a defining moment of favorable circumstance, with respect, honesty, love, and the space to explore life from God's perspective of me. Since that day, I have solidified my understanding of what it takes to be healed from abuse. As I look back on that moment, I am amazed at how God showed me my heart. I thought I had forgiven them all. My mouth had spoken it so eloquently over the years, but my heart was far from it. In my most vulnerable state amongst strangers, the Holy Spirit allowed me to transform my anger and hurt into healing and peace.

I beseech you, my brothers and sisters, if you're struggling with forgiveness, please understand that forgiveness is not for the person who hurt you—it's for you! Forgiveness will help you overcome feelings of depression, anxiety, and rage, as well as personal and relational conflicts. It is about making the conscious decision to let go of a grudge.

I struggled with it for years. How could I and why would I want to forgive someone who had caused me so much hurt and pain in the past? I couldn't let them off the hook that easy. I wanted them to hurt as badly as they had hurt me. But the moment God showed me my heart, I quickly realized it wasn't about them; it was about me setting myself free so that I could move forward in my own life. Someone once said to me, "You can forgive someone who wronged you and still call the police and testify in court."

Forgiveness requires a deep inquiry within ourselves about "our story." Forgiveness for me meant giving up the suffering of my past and being willing to forge ahead with far greater potential for inner freedom.

In this room full of women who had been hurting, I felt their pain. We were all speaking the same language, and not just English, but a language of repentance, a language of forgiveness, and a language of freedom! It was an amazing outpouring of our complete faith in the word of God that had spoken his teachings to us, individually and collectively, in the Sermon on the Mount: "Do good to them that hate you, and pray for them which despitefully use you."

My life's purpose is to help—to the best of my abilities—other women who were overcome by and are trying to heal from abuse. My purpose is to tell you, my sister, you may be broken, but GOD!

When you're in the thick of the pain from the abuse, it is very hard to believe that it will ever change; I am here to tell you, it does change and it does not take *forever*. When you reach the point of no return in life, situations that feel like there is no hope, run to God, stand on His promises for your life and don't give up. Cry out to the Creator and He will restore what was stolen from you. Allow God to fight your battles.

All my life tragedies had been wrestled to the ground, yet I still stood firm on the word of God to attest the authenticity of my faith. Although I had not always lived a life that was pleasing to God, I knew that He would never leave me nor would He forsake me. Even in my darkest hours, when I couldn't feel His presence or hear His voice, I knew He was there. Even when I centered my life around the men in my life and knew it wasn't pleasing to God, yet continued down a path of reckless disobedience, He was there. I had to go through hell and back and God had to break me to bring me to a place of total surrender.

I became like the woman at the well, who had been looking for love in all the wrong places. She had had five husbands and six men, and in the process of chasing all of them, she became empty. Nothing in the world will ever give us the satisfaction we long for except the unfailing love of God.

God's love for me is everlasting. Jeremiah 31:3 says, "The Lord hath appeared of old unto me, saying, Yea, I have loved thee with an everlasting love; therefore with lovingkindness have I drawn thee."

It is only when we surrender our whole hearts to Jesus Christ that we are restored and transformed. God will never extend our time of trouble beyond His purpose for us. And when God's purpose is to use you, He will first have to break you. I had been broken . . . but God.

It was the breaking of things that allowed me to see God. That's how it happened for the two on the road to Emmaus. They were walking along with Jesus for seven miles, talking to this man they knew like they knew their own faces, and yet didn't recognize Him. It was only when something got broken—the bread—that they recognized Jesus for who He was.

Nothing is broken that doesn't have a blessing behind it and a giving before it. Only by His Grace, only through Him and His way of providing, could I walk forward in courage. I am not taking any credit for this chapter in my life. It was not me, because that *me* would not have done this. I would have opted out of the story and refused to play a role.

I had been broken into a woman of genuine faith who survived and lived through every trial, every tribulation, and every season of my life. I survived because God had a purpose. I survived because I realized that I am not my past.

Don't allow your past to define who you are in Christ Jesus. Do not lose your identity in your circumstances or in other people; circumstances can shift and people can change or prove to be not who you thought, and when they do, they can leave you feeling empty and unworthy of love. No matter what it looks like and no matter what others say, you have not seen all that life has to offer. No one knows how your story will end but God, and He often saves His best for last. Revive your soul!

Romans 8:28 says, "And we know that all things work together for good to those who love God, to those who are the called according to His purpose.

My dear friends, just because the glare of the sun doesn't beam down on your face doesn't mean there is nothing left for you to do. We must be women of genuine faith. Faith, indwelling faith, faith that has lived in you through every trial, every tribulation, and every season of your life.

It is dangerous to lose your identity in your circumstances, which may leave you feeling empty and unfulfilled. God knows there are many things only a woman who is full of years and experience can contribute. Redefine your purpose, gather your belongings, keep on giving, and keep on living. No matter what age, you have not seen all that life has to offer. We must learn to resist the temptation to dwell in our past and stop allowing it to determine who we are today. Begin to declare and decree: "I overcame what happened yesterday! I survived what happened in my past. I am not what happened to me."

When I thought I was going to lose my mind—God kept me. By the grace of God, I'm still here. Through the trials of life, I made it. What the devil meant for evil—God used for His glory!

RESOURCES FOR VICTIMS AND SURVIVORS OF DOMESTIC VIOLENCE

NATIONAL CRISIS ORGANIZATIONS AND ASSISTANCE:

The National Domestic Violence Hotline
1-800-799-7233 (SAFE)
www.ndvh.org

National Dating Abuse Helpline
1-866-331-9474
www.loveisrespect.org

Americans Overseas Domestic Violence Crisis Center
International Toll-Free (24/7)
1-866-USWOMEN (879-6636)
www.866uswomen.org

National Child Abuse Hotline/Childhelp
1-800-4-A-CHILD (1-800-422-4453)
www.childhelp.org

Resources for Victims and Survivors of Domestic Violence

National Sexual Assault Hotline
1-800-656-4673 (HOPE)
www.rainn.org

National Suicide Prevention Lifeline
1-800-273-8255 (TALK)
www.suicidepreventionlifeline.org

National Center for Victims of Crime
National Resource Center on Domestic Violence
1-800-537-2238
www.nrcdv.org and www.vawnet.org

Futures Without Violence: The National Health Resource Center on Domestic Violence
1-888-792-2873
www.futureswithoutviolence.org

National Center on Domestic Violence, Trauma & Mental Health
1-312-726-7020 ext. 2011
www.nationalcenterdvtraumamh.org

CHILDREN

Childhelp USA/National Child Abuse Hotline
1-800-422-4453
www.childhelpusa.org

TEENS

Love Is Respect
Hotline: 1-866-331-9474
www.loveisrespect.org

Break the Cycle
202-824-0707
www.breakthecycle.org

Domestic Violence Initiative
(303) 839-5510/ (877) 839-5510
www.dviforwomen.org

Deaf Abused Women's Network (DAWN)
Email: Hotline@deafdawn.org
VP: 202-559-5366
www.deafdawn.org

PRAYER FOR SURVIVORS OF DOMESTIC ABUSE

Father God,

I come to You praying on behalf of all domestic violence victims, survivors, abusers, and anybody that has ever been affected by domestic violence.

Lord God, I pray that You will comfort our hearts, heal our wounds, and transform our brokenness.

Lord God, give us courage, wisdom, humility, and grace. Help us to extend Your amazing grace to those who have abused us. Forgive them Lord, and help us to forgive them as You forgive us.

Father God, in the name of Jesus we stand against all forms of abuse. We bind every evil spirit associated with abuse and cast those abusive spirits back into the pits of hell from which they came.

Lord, we command every demonic spirit that seeks to destroy our self-esteem, self-worth, self-respect, self-love, self-confidence, and hope in You; we cast them out in the name of Jesus.

Holy Spirit, we welcome You into our most secret places. Come sit and dwell in our most inner parts. Create in us a clean heart, oh God, and renew right spirits in us daily. Wash us, cleanse us, and make us whole again.

Lord, we speak healing, restoration, peace, and deliverance over every man and woman reading this book. Even to the abusers who will read this book, Lord, we bless them. We speak Your blessings over their lives, that they may repent and come to know You as their personal Lord and Savior. In Jesus' Name we pray. Amen.

PRAYER OF PROTECTION

Psalm 91 (NIV)

1 Whoever dwells in the shelter of the Most High
 will rest in the shadow of the Almighty.
2 I will say of the LORD, "He is my refuge and my fortress,
 my God, in whom I trust."
3 Surely he will save you
 from the fowler's snare
 and from the deadly pestilence.
4 He will cover you with his feathers,
 and under his wings you will find refuge;
 his faithfulness will be your shield and rampart.
5 You will not fear the terror of night,
 nor the arrow that flies by day,
6 nor the pestilence that stalks in the darkness,
 nor the plague that destroys at midday.

7 A thousand may fall at your side,
ten thousand at your right hand,
but it will not come near you.
8 You will only observe with your eyes
and see the punishment of the wicked.
9 If you say, "The LORD is my refuge,"
and you make the Most High your dwelling,
10 no harm will overtake you,
no disaster will come near your tent.
11 For he will command his angels concerning you
to guard you in all your ways;
12 they will lift you up in their hands,
so that you will not strike your foot against a stone.
13 You will tread on the lion and the cobra;
you will trample the great lion and the serpent.
14 "Because he loves me," says the LORD, "I will rescue him;
I will protect him, for he acknowledges my name.
15 He will call on me, and I will answer him;
I will be with him in trouble,
I will deliver him and honor him.
16 With long life I will satisfy him
and show him my salvation."

A PRAYER FOR ABUSERS

"And when you pray, do not be like the hypocrites, for they love to pray standing in the synagogues and on the street corners to be seen by others. Truly I tell you, they have received their reward in full. But when you pray, go into your room, close the door and pray to your Father, who is unseen. Then your Father, who sees what is done in secret, will reward you. And when you pray, do not keep on babbling like pagans, for they think they will be heard because of their many words. Do not be like them, for your Father knows what you need before you ask him.

"This, then, is how you should pray:

"'Our Father in heaven,
hallowed be your name,
your kingdom come,
your will be done,
on earth as it is in heaven.
Give us today our daily bread.
And forgive us our debts,
as we also have forgiven our debtors.
And lead us not into temptation,
but deliver us from the evil one.'

For if you forgive other people when they sin against you, your heavenly Father will also forgive you. But if you do not forgive others their sins, your Father will not forgive your sins." Matthew 6:5–15 NIV

Most Holy Father in heaven, I humbly ask that You honor this prayer on behalf of those who are known as abusers, who hurt others, the abused. It is true that many who inflict pain upon others have been hurt themselves. Only You and those who have been sinned against understand the source of discouragement, betrayal, and pain. Therefore, only You and those who have been hurt can work together to embrace healing and restoration. Only You can access the dark places within our souls to touch that which is hiding, festering, and causing inner turmoil—and fighting without.

Father, please touch the inner child within all of us who have been hurt by those who we once trusted. Seek out the anger that grew from pain and enlighten those who lash out that there is a better way to live. Help those who hate themselves to not destroy others who are made in Your image. Give them hope, and send your Holy Spirit to call upon each one to turn unto You and be healed. Show those who abuse, kill, maim, and spew forth venom that the source of their actions is hell—not heaven. Call upon those who have lost faith in You to renew—and allow the disbelievers to see the Light. In Jesus' Name. Amen.

AFFIRMATIONS FOR WOMEN WHO HAVE BEEN ABUSED

The light of God within me is producing perfect results in every phase of my life right now.

Lord, I give to You my fear and I trust You.

Father God, all I am is Yours.

I place myself in Your hands.

I accept God's blessings for me.

God loves me.

This is the day that the Lord hath made, I will rejoice and be glad in it.

Perfect love casts out fear.

I am fearfully and wonderfully made.

God in His almighty goodness is dissolving and removing all negative thoughts and actions from my world.

The Spirit of God is with me, upholding and sustaining me and making all things right.

I am worthy.

I am more than enough.

SOURCES

Unless otherwise indicated, scripture quotations are from the Holy Bible, King James Version. All rights reserved.

Scriptures marked ESV are taken from English Standard Version®. Copyright © 2001 by Crossway, a publishing ministry of Good News Publishers. All rights reserved.

Scriptures marked NIV are taken from the New International Version®. Copyright © 1973, 1978, 1984, 2011 by Biblica, Inc.™. All rights reserved.

Scriptures marked NKJV are taken from the New King James Version®. Copyright © 1982 by Thomas Nelson. All rights reserved.

CREATING DISTINCTIVE BOOKS
WITH INTENTIONAL RESULTS

We're a collaborative group of creative masterminds with a mission to produce high-quality books to position you for monumental success in the marketplace.

Our professional team of writers, editors, designers, and marketing strategists work closely together to ensure that every detail of your book is a clear representation of the message in your writing.

Want to know more?
Write to us at info@publishyourgift.com
or call (888) 949-6228

Discover great books, exclusive offers, and more at
www.PublishYourGift.com

Connect with us on social media

@publishyourgift

www.ingramcontent.com/pod-product-compliance
Lightning Source LLC
Chambersburg PA
CBHW071614080526
44588CB00010B/1133